THIS BOOK IS PRESENTED TO:

From:

Date:

For sale by the Superintendent of Documents, U.S. Government Printing Office
Internet: bookstore.gpo.gov Phone: toll free (866) 512-1800; DC area (202) 512-1800
Fax: (202) 512-2104 Mail: Stop IDCC, Washington, DC 20402-0001

ISBN 978-0-16-092382-1

The
Noncommissioned Officer
and Petty Officer

The
Noncommissioned Officer
and Petty Officer

BACKBONE
of the Armed Forces

National Defense University Press
Washington, D.C.
2014

Library of Congress Cataloging-in-Publication Data

The noncommissioned officer and petty officer : backbone of the armed forces.
    pages cm
    "Through the direction of the Office of the Senior Enlisted Advisor to the Chairman of the Joint Chiefs of Staff, this book was written by a team of enlisted leaders representing the U.S. Army, Marine Corps, Navy, Air Force, and Coast Guard with the participation and support of the National Defense University."
    1. United States—Armed Forces—Non-commissioned officers—History. 2. United States. Navy—Petty officers—History. 3. United States. Coast Guard—Petty officers—History. I. United States. Office of the Senior Enlisted Advisor to the Chairman of the Joint Chiefs of Staff. II. National Defense University Press.
    UB408.N66 2013
    355.3'38—dc23

                                                    2013048346

Book design by Chris Dunham, U.S. Government Printing Office
Cover concept by Hugo Cantu, U.S. Army Sergeants Major Academy

National Defense University Press
260 Fifth Avenue (Building 64)
Suite 2500
Fort Lesley J. McNair
Washington, DC 20319

NDU Press publications are sold by the U.S. Government Printing Office. For ordering information, call (202) 512–1800 or write to the Superintendent of Documents, U.S. Government Printing Office, Washington, D.C. 20402. For GPO publications online, access its Web site at: http://bookstore.gpo.gov.

Contents

Foreword

All of us who have served in uniform—from the newest recruits to four-star generals and admirals—have respected and learned from the outstanding men and women who wear the chevrons, anchors, and stripes of our noncommissioned officer and petty officer corps. We know them to have exceptional competence, professional character, and soldierly grit—they are exemplars of our Profession of Arms.

Through the nature of their charge, our force's mid-level enlisted corps bears tremendous responsibility for accomplishing the mission. Just as important, they uphold the moral obligation for the care and success of the men and women they lead.

The mid-grade enlisted force plays a unique role within the entire force. They are the frontline of our profession. They represent our values, behaviors, and character to our most junior ranks every day, no matter what transitions we face today or challenges we will face. Noncommissioned officers and petty officers also safeguard the voice of the enlisted force, informing senior leaders' decisions with candor and care.

Our noncommissioned officers and petty officers have chosen the uncommon life unique to all members of the Profession of Arms, a life of service and sacrifice, grounded in our sacred oath to defend the Constitution. I am enormously proud of them. Their honorable service on and off the battlefield has earned America's respect and trust. And the mutual trust they build with their subordinates, peers, and superiors enables them to be the Backbone of the Armed Forces.

To the intrepid noncommissioned officers and petty officers who will use this book to advance your careers and our profession, thank you for your service and for the example you provide to the force.

—Martin E. Dempsey

General, U.S. Army
18th Chairman of the Joint Chiefs of Staff

Preface

Shortly after I was sworn into office by the 18th Chairman of the Joint Chiefs in October 2011, the Chairman and I met for a discussion about the Profession of Arms—a topic important to any of us who honorably wear the cloth of the Nation. For quite some time before that, I had longed for a way to capture what our nation's noncommissioned officer corps is all about: why they are so trusted and empowered, the professional commitment to help achieve our nation's objectives, and the moral obligation to care for America's sons and daughters who serve in uniform. By the end of the conversation, we agreed that writing a book about the Armed Forces noncommissioned officer and petty officer was not only the right idea but also, perhaps even more compelling, long overdue. The basic concept was to produce a book of, by, and for noncommissioned officers and petty officers.

On December 17, 1777, General George Washington's army returned to winter quarters in Valley Forge, Pennsylvania, tired and with little strategic success in their fight against the professional British army. This period in Valley Forge proved critical for the fledgling army. General Washington recruited a former Prussian officer, Baron Friedrich Wilhelm Von Steuben, as Inspector General to strengthen the professionalism of the colonial army. Von Steuben's training objectives constituted the first written plan for standards, discipline, and duty for Washington's army, and he initiated the first training manual that outlined the duties and responsibilities of the noncommissioned officer. So in an important way, December 17 is considered the birthdate of America's noncommissioned officer corps.

To accomplish this rather huge endeavor, I assembled a select group of enlisted leaders, representing the five military Service branches,

National Guard, and special operations forces as the primary writing team. Managed by two co-leaders, this writing team was entrusted with a charge: to write a book that holistically defines the nature and calling of the U.S. Armed Forces noncommissioned officer and petty officer. Grounded in the Profession of Arms and distinctive in its own right, this book complements the Department of Defense's *The Armed Forces Officer*, as well as the Services' noncommissioned officer and petty officer doctrinal manuals. The writing team was charged to make certain that their work accurately captures the attributes and competencies of noncommissioned officers and petty officers across all Service branches through the lenses of both war and peace. It is not a "how to" or instructional manual. Rather, it is focused on defining and characterizing the noncommissioned officer and petty officer.

Teamwork is a bedrock operating principle from the first day of our military life cycle. The team of writers (listed in the acknowledgments) worked seamlessly to produce an inspiring book about who we are, what we do, and why we do it. They remained mindful of the differing Service cultures and identities, and they sought to avoid an inadvertent dilution of any particular Service's expectations or standards. Because the Navy and Coast Guard use the term *petty officer* rather than *noncommissioned officer*, the authors made a conscious decision to conjoin the terms and use the initialism *NCO/PO* in order to reflect the proud heritage of these enlisted leaders and their Service cultures.

This book seeks to inspire, validate, and ultimately resonate with every Soldier, Marine, Sailor, Airman, and Coastguardsman—past, present, and future. It aims to pay appropriate tribute to the contributions of NCOs/POs in each branch of the Armed Forces.

All of us who were involved in producing this book hope that it finds a spot on your nightstand, qualifies for a place on a commander's reading list, and becomes a standard text for the various enlisted leadership academies. We want the book to serve as a working tool to renew our commitment to our profession. We would like it to be read not only by serving and former NCOs/POs but also by all junior enlisted aspiring to become enlisted leaders. We would like it to be digested by our officer corps so that they may fully recognize what our enlisted leaders bring to the units and organizations in which they serve. We hope our military veterans will treasure this book as they look back with pride on their own service to the Nation. Finally, we hope that our comrades in arms in other nations, who are an important part of our history, will likewise benefit from reading this book.

As I reflect on all that our Servicemembers do in the defense of the Nation, I am extremely humbled by their dedication to duty and their sacrifice. These patriots, whom I have served alongside—and served— during my career, obligate themselves to lead, motivate, develop, and achieve.

As you read this book, I believe you will see that it encapsulates why our noncommissioned officers and petty officers still proudly carry the torch as the Backbone of our Armed Forces.

—Bryan B. Battaglia

Sergeant Major, U.S. Marines
Senior Enlisted Advisor to the Chairman
of the Joint Chiefs of Staff

Acknowledgments

Through the direction of the Office of the Senior Enlisted Advisor to the Chairman of the Joint Chiefs of Staff, this book was written by a team of enlisted leaders representing the U.S. Army, Marine Corps, Navy, Air Force, and Coast Guard with the participation and support of the National Defense University. This enduring project—to define and holistically characterize the role of the noncommissioned officer/petty officer in the Armed Forces—proved a daunting one but long overdue.

All members of the writing team, except one, were serving or retired NCOs/POs. They represented the Active and Reserve components, including the Army and Air National Guards. The military authors' specialties and backgrounds covered a wide array of conventional and special operations, each with extensive experience in Service, joint, and coalition formations during national crisis, war, and peace. Co-leaders and members of the writing team (with their organization affiliations when they worked on this project) are:

Co-leaders:
Chief Master Sergeant Curtis L. Brownhill, USAF (Ret.), *former U.S. Central Command Senior Enlisted Advisor*
Dr. Albert C. Pierce, *Professor of Ethics and National Security, National Defense University*

Writing team members:
Command Master Chief (SS/EXW) Donald B. Abele, USN, *Deputy Director, U.S. Navy Senior Enlisted Academy*

Command Chief Master Sergeant Reginald Edwards, USAF, *District of Columbia National Guard Senior Enlisted Leader*

Command Sergeant Major Richard Espinoza, USA, *District of Columbia National Guard, Land Component Command*

Master Gunnery Sergeant Andrew Hampton, USMC, *Second Marine Division, G3 Operations*

Master Sergeant James P. Horvath, USMC, *Joint Special Operations Forces Senior Enlisted Academy, Special Operations Command*

Master Sergeant Douglas J. Schmidt, USAF, *Instructional Systems Designer, NCO Academy Curriculum, Thomas N. Barnes Center for Enlisted Education*

Master Sergeant Joel C. Zecca, USA, *Director, U.S. Army Advanced Leader Course—Common Core (DL), United States Army Sergeants Major Academy*

Chief Petty Officer C.C. Clayton, USCG, *Public Affairs, Headquarters U.S. Coast Guard*

The members of the writing team wish to thank and commend several individuals and organizations for their outstanding contributions to this project:

NDU Press, especially Dr. Jeffrey D. Smotherman for his superb editing

General Richard B. Myers, USAF (Ret.), Command Sergeant Major Jeff Mellinger, USA (Ret.), Command Sergeant Major Mark Ripka, USA (Ret.), and Dr. Rick Swain for their executive review of the manuscript and offering invaluable suggestions for improving the book

GPO Creative Services, particularly Chris Dunham for his original design work and typesetting

Hugo Cantu of the U.S. Army Sergeants Major Academy for his talented graphic support and cover concept.

Sergeant First Class Leroy Petry, USA, awarded Medal of Honor in 2009 for actions in Afghanistan

Introduction
The Backbone of the Armed Forces

To be a member of the United States Armed Forces—to wear the uniform of the Nation and the stripes, chevrons, or anchors of the military Services—is to continue a legacy of service, honor, and patriotism that transcends generations. Answering the call to serve is to join the long line of selfless patriots who make up the Profession of Arms. This profession does not belong solely to the United States. It stretches across borders and time to encompass a culture of service, expertise, and, in most cases, patriotism. Today, the Nation's young men and women voluntarily take an oath to support and defend the Constitution of the United States and fall into formation with other proud and determined individuals who have answered the call to defend freedom. This splendid legacy, forged in crisis and enriched during times of peace, is deeply rooted in a time-tested warrior ethos. It is inspired by the notion of contributing to something larger, deeper, and more profound than one's own self.

Strengthened by the diversity of its citizens, the United States remains a global vanguard of freedom, democracy, human rights, and opportunity. The monumental task of keeping the Nation secure, protecting its citizens, and assisting in crisis across the globe often falls on the shoulders of the United States Armed Forces. Comprised of Active-duty, Reserve, and National Guard components, today's all-volunteer Total Force is led by committed and trusted leaders—officers and noncommissioned officers (NCOs)/petty officers (POs) who embody the discipline, intellect, and fortitude needed to support our national security strategy and help achieve its national objectives. Theirs is a solemn obligation fortified by the sacred trust of the American people. This trust looks not only for well-planned execution of military operations and responsible management of national resources, but also for the care of its most precious treasure—America's sons and daughters.

At the beginning of this project, the writing team crafted a paragraph to define and characterize NCOs/POs. The book drew its shape and focus from this original paragraph:

> *As an enlisted member in the Armed Forces of the United States, you are a member of the Profession of Arms and have taken an oath of enlistment to support and defend the Constitution. When you become a Noncommissioned Officer or Petty Officer, you are then an empowered and trusted leader in America's all-volunteer force. As a leader and technical expert, you enhance organizational effectiveness and directly contribute to mission success. Innovative, adaptive, and resilient, you are the indispensable link between command guidance and execution, ensuring that each task is fully understood and supervised through completion. You are responsible and accountable for the development and welfare of your subordinates. You teach, coach, and mentor them. As a steward of the institution, you enforce its standards and are its ambassador to the world.*

The writing team concluded that NCOs/POs are the bridging leaders within every Service branch. The dual roles of NCOs/POs may be best described as "complement the officer, enable the force." How both are done by the NCO/PO is much more art than science. The collective capacity of the NCO/PO ranks, junior to senior, forms a distinct and invaluable leadership cadre that balances artfully between mission and people. NCOs/POs possess professional qualities, competencies, and traits that complement the officer corps and enable the enlisted force. They are trusted and empowered leaders in the Profession of Arms— the Backbone of the Armed Forces.

This book aims to define and illustrate who NCOs/POs are, what they do, and why they are a critical enabler within the Armed Forces.

Each chapter builds upon concepts and foundations from other chapters, offering a continuity of core ideas. If the authors have been successful, the audience should conclude not only that NCOs/POs are bona fide members of the Profession of Arms, but also that, given their extraordinary roles and responsibilities, NCOs/POs are quintessential leaders within the profession.

The clear evolution of NCOs/POs, from traditional supporting figures to empowered and integrated leaders, spans all five military Services. It is a product of thoughtful institutional investment and the remarkable accomplishments over centuries of service. Today's NCOs/POs benefit tangibly from the legacy of those who served before. As a result of their predecessors' deeds and remarkable successes, today's NCOs/POs serve both in ways their predecessors would still recognize and in ways almost unimaginable only a few decades ago. With one eye on the past and one on the future, the Armed Forces have re-evaluated the knowledge, skills, and abilities of enlisted leadership and adapted them for current and future requirements, yielding today's professional enlisted force. As an outcome of this evolutionary effort, NCOs/POs are now empowered to assume added roles and responsibilities—with commensurate accountability—once reserved for the commissioned officer corps in each Service.

American NCOs/POs are distinctive in the global Profession of Arms. This is a result of their common professional education, training, and development. *NCOs/POs are expected to do the right thing for the right reasons, irrespective of influence, complexity, or urgency.* This high degree of trust and confidence is institutionalized within the Armed Forces by both superior officers and the enlisted men and women whom NCOs/POs are responsible for developing and leading.

General James N. Mattis, USMC (Ret.), aptly described why the Nation needs its Armed Forces: "We're going to have to fight to defend this experiment we call 'America,' to see if a government of the people, by the people and for the people can survive in an inhospitable environment. If we want the values that grew out of the Enlightenment to survive, we're going to have to fight." This means to fight for the Nation and to maintain the honor and reputation of the Profession of Arms. The lineage of the Profession of Arms and the Armed Forces of the United States has been fortified by millions of uniformed men and women. Many have paid the price of anguish, pain, blood, limb, and life. And many others carry invisible scars from the weight of war, conflict, and service around the globe.

America's corps of enlisted leaders and its longstanding reputation have been forged by patriotic men and women maintaining unwavering standards during extraordinary times, and by those who have carried the colors forward into past battles, campaigns, and wars on behalf of the Nation. The "Gold Star" mother, who has endured the immense burden of sacrifice within her family, must find comfort in the knowledge that her country's Armed Forces will continue to protect the Nation from tyranny and oppression, and that her son or daughter was entrusted to and led by the finest leaders, the noncommissioned officers and petty officers.

Ultimately, this book belongs to the U.S. military's noncommissioned officers and petty officers—past, present, and future. With great respect and admiration to those who have ever worn—and to those who aspire to wear—stripes, chevrons, or anchors, the dedicated writing team humbly presents this book as an inspiring testament about the Backbone of the Armed Forces.

James Cox

Fighting with 2nd Infantry Division north of the Chongchon River, Sergeant First Class Major Cleveland, weapons squad leader, points out communist-led North Korean position to his machinegun crew, November 20, 1950

CHAPTER ONE

Noncommissioned Officers/ Petty Officers: Who They Are, What They Do

As we finished another evening meal at this forward operating base, I was drawn to a familiar commotion. A U.S. Army gun truck team led by a staff sergeant arrived barely in time to catch a late dinner. It was obvious this team had just returned from another grueling combat mission on the road. They looked tired, tattered, and hungry. Still wearing full body armor and carrying their rifles properly slung and secured, they made their way to the meal line. The NCO stayed back, allowing his team to get their meals and eat first. As the most junior ranking member, a private first class, passed him, the sergeant placed a comforting hand on the young man's shoulder and asked, "Hanging in there, Adams?" "Hooah, staff sergeant," the Soldier replied reassuringly as he grabbed a tray and utensils. The staff sergeant was the last to join his team at their table. They enjoyed a brief time of comradeship as he quickly scoffed down his meal, and within minutes, began gathering his equipment. Standing back up, he informed the men that he was off to brief battalion, placing his next ranking sergeant in charge, and leaving in a hurry.

I often find myself thinking back to that deployment and to that evening. I admired the solidarity and cohesion that existed among that gun truck unit and the comportment of that NCO. It was apparent to me that he was the mainstay of that team. He demonstrated competence, confidence, and a tireless sense of duty to his cause, his command, and his comrades in arms. He placed the needs and well-being of his team ahead of his own, without sacrificing established standards, discipline, or ethical behavior. He served not only as a leader to his men, but a follower to his leadership. He embodied the strength, versatility, selflessness, grit, and dedication of the enlisted military professional, and he personified the reason why noncommissioned officers and petty officers are, indeed, the Backbone of the U.S. Armed Forces.

This personal account from a senior noncommissioned officer who observed the scene is just one depiction of the noncommissioned officer/petty officer in action, as seen through the eyes of a fellow Servicemember. Similar stories of NCO/PO dedication are found in the memories of veterans of World War II, the Korean War, the Vietnam War, and other conflicts of the 20th and 21st centuries. Not all of these stories unfold in a war zone; some occurred in stateside barracks, on ships in homeport, and at airbases around the globe. But what do they have in common?

Regardless of Service, every NCO/PO shares a core essence and ancestry grounded in ready obedience, selfless dedication, and uncompromising integrity. As stewards of the enlisted force, NCOs/POs serve as protectors, guides, and guardians to America's sons and daughters who have committed themselves to defending the Constitution, as well as the Nation's values, freedoms, and way of life. They are responsible for developing, preparing, sustaining, and advancing the enlisted force to meet the challenges of the 21st-century global security environment. Whether viewed through the eyes of a fellow enlisted Servicemember, commissioned officer, retired veteran, citizen of a foreign nation, parent, spouse, or child, today's NCOs/POs are the quintessential leaders to their subordinates, loyal followers to their leaders, and an inspiration to all.

The Servant-Leader

The Armed Forces preserve a legacy of loyalty, honor, commitment, and perseverance that has stood the test of time and the hardships of conflict and chaos. A deeper look reveals the rich history of the NCO/

PO in shouldering immense responsibility as trusted leaders and serving proudly at the forefront. The trust, granted by their commands and witnessed by the American people, relies on their conduct and character to ensure that the members of the Armed Forces perform to the standards expected of them. As empowered leaders of the enlisted force, NCOs/POs are in the most advantageous position to influence, motivate, and develop their Soldiers, Marines, Sailors, Airmen, and Coastguardsmen so that they enthusiastically *want* to work toward and achieve the goals established for the common good. As disciplined and devoted professionals, they follow orders and faithfully carry out responsibilities while ensuring that they themselves, and the men and women in their charge, comply with all laws and regulations and exercise sound moral reasoning to ensure highly ethical conduct.

From the most junior NCO/PO to the most senior enlisted advisors across the five Service branches, NCOs/POs are skilled and professional leaders, critical to all levels of military organization and command. While all those who have successfully completed initial military training have proudly earned the title of Soldier, Marine, Sailor, Airman, or Coastguardsman, NCOs/POs are the specially trusted leaders who provide an indispensable and irreplaceable linkage between command guidance and mission execution. They are the competent, credible, and capable servant-leaders who influence and impact every aspect of an organization's operations, administration, and climate. They embody and enforce high standards and live by an austere code of conduct, maintaining an ethical and moral high ground and unwavering dedication to duty. A true and devoted NCO/PO is the embodiment of responsibility and accountability, never shirking his duty.

As technical and functional experts, specialized practitioners, and advisors steeped in tactics, techniques, and procedures, NCOs/POs carry out both the art and the science of the Profession of Arms. Subordinates and commanders alike draw upon enlisted leaders' expertise and experience to achieve mission objectives and depend on them as leaders and managers. NCOs/POs are expected to acquire and employ applicable resources efficiently and effectively, to think critically to prevent and solve problems. Moreover, they must be able to communicate continually up, down, and across Service, joint, and coalition chains of command. They accrue extensive practical experience and specialized training, professional military education, and mentoring, all of which further enhance their capabilities. It is through this dynamic process of development and maturation that NCOs/POs emerge from the ranks as the most seasoned Servicemembers capable of not only leading the enlisted force of today but also developing military leaders for tomorrow.

Heroic and righteous acts of selfless physical and moral courage highlight the history and fidelity of the NCO/PO—sometimes incredible deeds performed for the sake of their fellow Servicemembers, their nation, and its vital interests. But NCOs/POs contribute every day, in ways small and large, obvious and subtle, in war and in peace, overseas and at home. Each action, decision, and behavior is a reflection of that individual military member's character and professionalism. NCOs/POs cultivate the virtues of decency, fairness, honesty, humility, integrity, and valor through their own actions—by walking the walk, not simply talking the talk. They play a vital role in upholding the tradition and image of the Profession of Arms by instilling its noble qualities in others. It is the skill and character of NCOs/POs that earn the admiration, trust, and respect of their subordinates, peers, superiors, and the American people.

The will to serve in the U.S. military is ignited by an unmatched desire to safeguard the life, liberty, and freedom that all Americans cherish, and others may envy. The patriotic flame that burns within every Servicemember is sometimes threatened and can occasionally flicker from the rigors and realities of the arduous lifestyle in the U.S. military, but it will never be extinguished. America's military serves around the world, often in uncertain and dangerous situations far from the comforts of home. Such circumstances test resilience, will, and wits. Commanders and subordinates alike count on the expertise and perseverance of their NCOs/POs to ensure that the enlisted force is physically and mentally prepared to face the rigors and challenges of high-tempo operations and expeditionary environments, as well as seeing to the more routine yet important work of providing training, maintenance, and professional development of subordinates. NCOs/POs nurture individual and organizational well-being by genuinely caring for their subordinates and promoting morale and esprit de corps within their units. They demonstrate compassion, empathy, and support for fellow Servicemembers and their families who may be struggling with adversity and loss. They foster programs and activities that promote camaraderie, a healthy social support network, and a sense of belonging within and beyond their organizations.

NCOs/POs in the Organization

Noncommissioned officers/petty officers are the leadership cadre that ensures the mission of the unit or organization can and will be accomplished. They do so by sustaining and motivating the enlisted force. By teaching, coaching, and mentoring the force, and by instilling a sense of unity, purpose, good order, and discipline—and demanding compliance with standards, tradition, culture, customs, and courtesies—they are looked upon as the organization's pillars of strength and loyalty. They are professional servant-leaders who are undeterred by the chaos, complexity, uncertainty, fog, and friction that can infiltrate the formations. They have presence. When young military members look up from a difficult task for purpose, strength, and guidance, it is the NCO/PO they see first. NCOs/POs continually strive to attain ever higher levels of personal, professional, and technical competence in order to be more effective, and they inspire confidence and esprit de corps both in those appointed over them and in those who look to them for leadership. NCOs/POs influence and develop their subordinates through personal example and engaged supervision. NCOs/POs relish taking on challenging tasks—that is what they are developed for and trained to do, and it is one of the many reasons they are acknowledged and respected throughout the world.

The traits, qualities, and competencies that NCOs/POs develop within their respective Services enable them to carry out their fundamental roles and responsibilities as the team-builders, force-multipliers, problem-solvers, implementers, and enforcers who take plans and orders from concept to completion. They lead and execute assigned and implied tasks competently, without hesitation. The collective capacity of the NCO/PO ranks, junior to senior, represents a formidable leadership cadre that adds value to the organization. Because they are the leaders closest to the force, NCOs/POs have the greatest effect on accomplishing organizational goals and achieving mission success.

They help to keep the organization functioning by maintaining open and effective support channels, while efficiently conducting day-to-day operations within the framework of prescribed policies and directives. Most importantly, they prepare the organization for its wartime mission. NCOs/POs neither relinquish what is right nor allow deviations from law, policies, command guidance, and established standards. At the same time, they are expected to display insight and exercise sound judgment and common sense, as well as ingenuity and innovation. They take the necessary risks and are confident in seeking out the inputs of the team, realizing that at times the most effective ideas can come from a subordinate closer to the problem.

NCOs/POs are a commander's treasure, a source of seasoned perspectives that transcends place in the organizational hierarchy, a place neatly balanced between mission and people. They provide the commander and officer corps with unique insights and actionable perspectives while also providing an enlisted voice in matters concerning operations, administration, readiness, and the well-being of the force. They contribute directly to the development of organizational goals, objectives, and courses of action that enhance operational effectiveness. Furthermore, NCOs/POs convey an essential element of experience (art) as well as skills and competencies (science) on all matters concerning organizational capacity and command climate. They are the trusted counselors for the commissioned leaders, enhancing the officers' abilities to lead and/or command effectively.

The officer-NCO/PO relationship is one of the hallmarks of the Armed Forces and a key element in unit effectiveness. Examples include:

- pilot and crew chief
- division officer and leading petty officer
- platoon leader and platoon sergeant
- section officer-in-charge and chief petty officer
- flight commander and flight chief
- company commander and first sergeant
- maintenance officer and superintendent
- cutter commanding officer and collateral duty unit command chief

- submarine captain and chief of the boat
- regimental commander and sergeant major
- brigade commander and command sergeant major
- wing commander and command chief master sergeant
- fleet commander and fleet master chief petty officer
- combatant commander and command senior enlisted leader
- Service chief and Service senior enlisted advisor
- Chairman of the Joint Chiefs of Staff and Senior Enlisted Advisor to the Chairman.

Empowered

NCOs/POs across all Services and domains are accountable for their personal actions, as well as for the actions of their subordinates. They are empowered with responsibilities and authorities to maintain good order and discipline at all times. Even after normal duty hours, on weekends, and on holidays, when NCOs/POs are out of uniform, they remain NCOs/POs. They must carry out all obligatory and entrusted responsibilities to ensure that standards, obedience, and discipline are upheld *at all times*, both by themselves and any Servicemember within sight or hearing. Furthermore, they are never "off duty" when it comes to the well-being of their subordinates. Even at 0200 hours on a weekend, the NCO/PO does not hesitate to respond to a subordinate's crisis.

NCOs/POs are provided certain legal authorities that support their abilities to maintain good order and discipline of the force supporting the command's mission. Under the Uniform Code of Military Justice (UCMJ), Article 91 provides for punishment for insubordinate conduct toward any warrant officer, noncommissioned officer, or petty officer. Additionally, Article 92 provides for punishment for failure to obey an order or regulation. The NCO/PO may also be delegated authorities by the commander, which are dependent on Service doctrine, organizational position, and predetermined levels of responsibility and accountability. For example, a Coast Guard master chief petty officer, while serving as an officer-in-charge of a river tender, would have nonjudicial punishment authority over the crew unless it is withheld by a superior authority. The *Manual for Courts-Martial* allows commanders to empower NCOs/POs with administering extra-military instruction (also known as extra training) to subordinates who need additional tutelage and development.

Regardless of Service branch or category, the UCMJ authorizes all noncommissioned officers/petty officers in the official performance of their duties to place any individual under military apprehension who appears to be in violation of the code. These examples of empowerment and authority are not taken lightly and are one of the many tools that make the U.S. enlisted leader unique from other nations' militaries.

While there may be profound differences among the Services in doctrine, culture, and identity, the various enlisted creeds all convey the key qualities of leadership, allegiance, competence, and responsibility to the profession, to the organization's senior leadership, and to the men and women under their charge. The various Service creeds charge NCOs/POs to lead, develop, and inspire others to support and defend the Constitution, keep the Nation secure, and uphold the standards of their charters (see appendix C).

The formal chain of command is a foundational feature of any military organization. It establishes lines of authority and communication at each echelon and assigns requisite levels of responsibility and accountability for the conduct of day-to-day operations for the organization's garrison and wartime mission. The chain of command promotes unity of purpose by facilitating an efficient communications process for commanders to convey their guidance and intent (statement of purpose) to the members of the organization, thus ensuring their orders are passed down accurately and carried out effectively. It provides a means for members of the unit to raise their concerns, achieve clarity in complex issues, and resolve problems. NCOs/POs are an invaluable and essential link in the chain of command. They add value and purpose at every level, and as a leadership cadre they ensure the organization remains strong and responsive.

Accountability is a keystone principle of the Profession of Arms. It is intrinsic to each echelon of the chain of command. It ensures that orders will be carried out and mission objectives will be achieved. Integral to unity of command, accountability is related directly to positional responsibility and is deeply rooted in trust and confidence. Each Service places extraordinary trust and confidence in its NCO/PO corps, knowing that mission accomplishment and the lives of others are at stake. Trust and confidence can be observed commonly in the synchronized and professional relationships between officers and NCOs/POs. In the absence of a commissioned officer in charge, the experienced NCO/PO is assumed to possess the positional authority, qualifications, and ability to step in and lead the mission. This concept is an essential component of U.S. military doctrine and is vital to each Service's expectations for its NCOs/POs. If the platoon leader becomes incapacitated, the platoon sergeant assumes command through mission completion or relief by higher authority. The trust and confidence that officers have in NCOs/POs can be seen in countless instances when a mission, operation, activity, or effort must continue in the absence of the otherwise responsible officer.

Given their experience and ability to influence and guide others, NCOs/POs are a decisive factor in the force's ability to forge ahead through friction points, adversity, and uncertainty in order to accomplish the mission. They do so by maintaining a high degree of situational awareness and by keeping the force informed of mission purpose, unit contribution, and overall effect. NCOs/POs understand mission objectives and are adept at clarifying and accurately conveying the commander's guidance and intent in the face of changing conditions. They do this in meaningful words with a self-assured manner that in turn instills confidence in the force and provides an azimuth to success. Effective organizational communications (vertical and horizontal) require openness, inclusiveness, approachability, and an ability to translate abstract issues into concrete and meaningful terms. Their distinctive know-how also enables NCOs/POs to make sound recommendations and develop and convey effective courses of action vital to any high-performing organization. Perhaps the essence of NCO/PO organizational communication may be summed up in the answers to three questions: "What do I know? Who needs to know? Have I told them—with a sense of urgency?"

The noteworthy contributions of NCOs/POs fully support and sustain the standards of the Profession of Arms. They are competent, credible, and capable leaders who pledge themselves to the profession, embody its ethos, and develop and influence others to adhere to a selfless calling of service. With commissioned officers, NCOs/POs lead the force to provide for the common defense. They are particularly responsible for the lives and welfare of their most precious charge—the men and women they lead. NCOs/POs preserve the integrity of the profession by keeping a discerning eye on compliance and discipline, and they perform a critical role in policing the ranks as well as developing future leaders.

Force development and sustainment are paramount leadership priorities for NCOs/POs. They impress upon the force that the principal requirement of the Profession of Arms is the ethical and effective application of the military element of national power. They teach, coach, and mentor their subordinates in the art and science of armed conflict. NCOs/POs help maintain a high quality force by ensuring that a healthy and positive environment exists for all members. They are intimately involved in appraising the performance of the enlisted personnel under their supervision and, when appropriate, recommending them for retention, grade advancement, increased levels of responsibility, or even discharge. They also advance the enlisted force by contributing to the individual development of subordinates, conducting enlisted professional military education programs at each level, and fostering a continuous learning environment for both professional and personal development. While their primary focus and efforts are placed on leading and developing the enlisted force, NCOs/POs do contribute significantly to the development of junior and midgrade officers as well because of their knowledge, experience, and insights.

The Profession of Arms is unique in the sense that even the longest military career is short compared to most other recognized professions. Relatively young NCOs/POs lead a dynamic force that includes a disproportionate share of even younger, less experienced men and women. As the stewards of the institution, NCOs/POs ensure continuity of military traditions, culture, identity, standards, and methods of operating as new generations fall into formation. By exercising the principle of bridging the basics, the NCO/PO perpetuates the legacy of service by the increasingly bright, committed, and capable future generations who will proudly wear the cloth of the Nation. No matter what their age or experience, all members of the Profession of Arms will follow an engaged NCO/PO who works tirelessly to enhance the effectiveness of the organization—and who genuinely cares for and appreciates the contributions and sacrifices of its members.

Few volunteer to serve the Nation in the Armed Forces, and even fewer are selected to be its trusted leaders. NCOs/POs carry out this enormous responsibility by maintaining a unique balance between mission and people, along with steadfast commitment and vigor that neither waver nor yield in the face of uncertainty or complexity.

Serving as an NCO/PO is not for the faint of heart. It is a daunting responsibility and a way of life that calls for substantial sacrifice and unfailing loyalty. Despite all this, the men and women who wear these ranks do so with boundless discipline, obedience, commitment, and enthusiasm. From the inception of the Continental Army in 1775 to the collective capacity of the interoperable Armed Forces today, America's NCOs/POs have established their legacy as servant-leaders. An indispensable link between mission command and execution, they serve as force enablers leading by example. Our nation's citizens look to the Armed Forces as the vanguard of freedom and to its noncommissioned officers/petty officers as the Backbone of that force.

Captain Bruce H. Lindsey, left, commanding officer of the USS Carl Vinson *(CVN 70), administers Oath of Enlistment to Sailors during a ceremony at the USS* Arizona *Memorial in Joint Base Pearl Harbor–Hickam, Hawaii, June 9, 2011. The Sailors are, left to right, Quartermaster 1st Class Reed T. Gonzales, Aviation Ordnanceman 3rd Class John C. Anthony, Information Systems Technician 2nd Class Sarah M. Peachey, and Aviation Machinist's Mate 1st Class Jason C. Evans*

CHAPTER TWO

The Profession of Arms: An Ancient and Honorable Tradition

The Profession of Arms is much older than our young country. The profession emerged over the centuries, arising from the need to defend a nation's territory, culture, ideals, and people. Its members were the noble few who stood for what was morally right and ethically just, who endured the burdens, and who fought to defend their nation's interests or to shield those who could not protect themselves:

> *From the beginning of man's recorded history physical force, or the threat of it, has always been freely applied to the resolution of social problems. The function of the profession of arms is the ordered application of force in the resolution of a social problem. It has evolved into a profession, not only in the wider sense of what is professed, but in the narrower sense of an occupation with a distinguishable corpus of specific technical knowledge and doctrine, a more or less exclusive group coherence, a complex of institutions peculiar to itself, an educational pattern adapted to its own specific needs, a career structure of its own and a distinct place in the society which has brought it forth.*[1]

Those who answer this call and embody the warrior spirit are the few who are prepared to give what President Abraham Lincoln described as their "last full measure of devotion" in order to serve a higher cause.[2]

The Profession of Arms in the United States

Those who proudly wear the uniforms of the U.S. Armed Forces are steeped in that broader history and tradition, but they are also the inheritors of the unique tradition of the Profession of Arms in the United States that dates back to the earliest days of the Republic, and in the case of the National Guard units, beyond. Before the American Revolution, colonial towns mustered a militia when needed. At the onset of the Revolutionary War, the 13 colonies had only militias comprised of more or less unskilled troops to defend against a professionally trained British army. Once the war began, the Continental Congress created a Continental Army on June 14, 1775, and established an initial enlistment of 1 year. Later, when the Founding Fathers wrote the Preamble to the Constitution, they identified the fundamental requirements of a national government. Providing for the common defense was fourth among them:

> *We the People of the United States, in Order to form a more perfect Union, establish Justice, insure domestic Tranquility, provide for the common defence, promote the general Welfare, and secure the Blessings of Liberty to ourselves and our Posterity, do ordain and establish this Constitution for the United States of America.*[3]

Article I, Section 8, and Article II, Section 2, provide the constitutional framework for the Armed Forces of the United States. The Army, Marine Corps, and Navy predate the Constitution. The Coast Guard came a bit later, and the Air Force emerged in 1947 as a separate Service after World War II. Though young compared to some allied militaries, the U.S. military has formally existed for over two centuries. The U.S. Armed Forces have continually evolved through advancements in education, training, and professional development.

On his first day as the 18th Chairman of the Joint Chiefs of Staff, General Martin E. Dempsey wrote a letter to the Joint Force in which he addressed his view on the Profession of Arms in the United States: "We must renew our commitment to the Profession of Arms. We're not a profession simply because we say we're a profession. We must continue to learn, to understand, and to promote the knowledge, skills, attributes, and behaviors that define us as a profession."[4]

But what constitutes a profession? A profession is made up of practitioners performing a kind of knowledge-based work in which the workers enjoy a high degree of independence in application of particular skills. A profession generally has four basic elements: a specialized practical expertise, an acknowledged responsibility to society, a sense of corporateness, and a professional ethos.[5]

First, a profession possesses a specialized body of theoretical and practical knowledge developed through extensive education, training, and experience. The military's core expertise is in the ethical application of force on behalf of the Nation. This work of developing and conveying a body of knowledge takes place in military schoolhouses throughout a career. This learning journey is guided by an established or "doctrinal" plan of continuous education and professional development that unfolds as one advances in the profession. As the operating environment evolves and technology advances, the learning process must adapt.

Second, a profession has an acknowledged responsibility to provide an important and specialized service to the larger society. In the case of the medical profession, the service is preserving and enhancing the health of the population. In the Profession of Arms, it is providing for "the common defence" by prevention and deterrence of war and, if necessary, facing adversaries through kinetic and nonkinetic means in order to achieve national objectives. Every profession has, in effect, a compact with the larger society. Society grants the profession certain powers, privileges, and prerogatives not normally granted to others; in exchange, the profession provides reliable and longstanding service to society. Most particularly, members of professions are granted wide discretionary latitude in performance of their specialized duties.

Third, a profession generally has a sense of corporateness, a shared sense of mutual identity. This includes having a formally recognized role in determining, within limits, who may enter the profession and who may remain in it. Members of the profession certify and credential individual professionals at appropriate levels of competence within their specialized fields of knowledge. The levels of certification and expertise often reflect the progression within a profession. This progression reflects the older notion of apprentice, journeyman, and master. This certification is seen at every skill level within military occupational specialties, as well as in professional military education institutions for both specialized and general skills.

The fourth and final element of a profession is that it generally has a commonly accepted ethos, an ethical framework or code that guides and governs the behavior of its membership. The ethos binds members together in a common calling. The Profession of Arms shares a warrior ethos. The fundamental ideals and virtues of the Profession of Arms transcend time and cultures. Among these, but not all inclusive, are discipline, courage, honor, loyalty, duty, integrity, and endurance. In the United States, the members of this noble profession are held to a higher standard of conduct than most of their fellow citizens. They are required to follow a unique set of laws and a code that guides them morally and ethically, while preparing for—and during—the heat of battle. This code is what separates them from mere criminals, savages, mercenaries, and terrorists. They bear arms and share risks out of necessity at the call of their nation, not out of enjoyment or uncivilized greed. For U.S. military personnel, the requirements of the Uniform Code of Military Justice, the six articles of the U.S. Armed Forces Code of Conduct, and the respective Service creeds and core values guide and govern professional behavior. The Oath of Enlistment formalizes the commitment each military member assumes:

> I, _____, do solemnly swear (or affirm) that I will support and defend the Constitution of the United States against all enemies, foreign and domestic; that I will bear true faith and allegiance to the same; and that I will obey the orders of the President of the United States and the orders of the officers appointed over me, according to regulations and the Uniform Code of Military Justice. So help me God.[6]

The Oath of Enlistment has endured the test of time as a public acknowledgment of an obligation to support and defend the Constitution at all costs. The first pre-constitutional oath was established by the Continental Congress during the Revolutionary War to enlist men into the Continental Army. Our forefathers saw the need for an oath to renounce any residual obligations of allegiance to King George III and to ensure loyalty to the newly formed Continental Congress. Two oaths were established on June 14, 1775, one for enlisted and one for officers. The enlisted oath has slightly evolved over time, but the power within the message has remained consistent. Pronounced aloud, it is a public manifestation of the solemn commitment each military member makes to support and defend the Constitution. The swearing of the oath is done ceremonially. Traditionally, there is a U.S. flag at the site, and upon conclusion of the oath, there is a handshake of congratulations between the administering officer and the enlistee. The flag represents the Nation the new military member promises to serve.

Those who take this oath share a bond of dedication and service in which they legitimately take great pride. The first Senior Enlisted Advisor to the Chairman of the Joint Chiefs of Staff, Command Sergeant Major William Gainey, USA, spoke of this pride in remarks to a group of noncommissioned officers: "You are the people who give this country and its people their freedoms. . . . Always remember when people ask you what you do for a living to hold your head up high, look them square in the eye, and say with pride 'I'm in the military.' Pride is contagious."[7]

Out of our entire nation and its territories, only a small percentage of citizens answer the call to enlist as members of the Profession of Arms. Since 1973, they have done so voluntarily. Servicemembers near the end of their contract, if the nature of their service warrants it, have the ability to re-enlist and renew their commitment. This usually has a reinvigorating effect on the Servicemembers, their comrades in arms, and their families. The individual Services re-enlist their members, but they *retain* their families. Re-enlistment is a reciprocal display of trust and cohesion between the military family and the Service, as both of them share the member.

NCOs/POs play an important role in the re-enlistment process. They act as moral guides and help junior enlisted Servicemembers balance the demands of life, family, and the continuous commitment to the Nation. They are the eyes and ears of their commanders and have a responsibility to the readiness of the organization. They have a relevant say in who is best qualified for continued service. This is another dimension of the special bond and relationship between the NCO/PO and officer. NCOs/POs mentor junior enlisted Servicemembers and participate in the retention decisionmaking process.

Re-enlisting and renewing the commitment is a very special occasion. Servicemembers traditionally get to pick where and how they want to re-enlist. Some have held their ceremonies aboard aircraft and then rappelled or parachuted out, some re-enlist underwater, others on the battlefield, and some even at sports arenas in front of thousands and perhaps millions. The honor and privilege of re-enlisting is just as sacred to the re-enlisting official as it is to the re-enlisting member.

The Oath of Enlistment is the public agreement that allows one to enter or re-enter this age-old profession. Since the beginning of the Nation, millions have publicly professed, sworn, or affirmed the Oath of Enlistment. The oath is a legal and binding agreement that is the prerequisite to becoming a member of the Armed Forces. Service is a calling, a vocation that only a small percentage of our nation will accept in their lifetimes. Noncommissioned officers/petty officers fully understand what it means to be a member of the Profession of Arms and the Armed Forces of the United States.

The Journey in the Profession

Former Sergeant Major of the Army Kenneth Preston described his profession aptly: "Just as other professions have entry level or apprentice, mid-level or journeyman, and senior or expert levels within their professions, we have levels of competence within our Army."[8] After swearing/affirming the Oath of Enlistment, one has legally provided a verbal and written commitment to the U.S. Government and its people. Certification and testing to become a full-fledged professional member of the Armed Forces are achieved upon completion of specific basic training/boot camp where one earns the prestigious title of Soldier, Marine, Sailor, Airman, or Coastguardsman. Upon graduation and attaining that military-specific professional designation, individuals have earned the basic certification as members of the Profession of Arms. The next step in the journey is to progress to military occupational specialty/rate training, after which apprentice professionals move onto their first duty stations or ships, or if they are members of the U.S. Armed Forces Reserve component, into a Reserve/National

Guard unit where they will complete skill training and begin to build experience that will lead them to become journeymen, and potentially masters, in the Profession of Arms.

Achieving credentials and certifications for military specialties through either formal schooling or on the job training is challenging. The profession demands it be that way because excellence is the standard. A vital part of reaching that standard is the presence of engaged NCOs/POs at all levels. They are the leaders empowered by their chain of command and trusted by the American people to uphold and enforce the standards of the Profession of Arms.

Notes

[1] General Sir John Winthrop Hackett, *The Profession of Arms* (New York: Macmillan, 1983), 9.

[2] Abraham Lincoln, "Address Delivered at the Dedication of the Cemetery at Gettysburg, 19 November 1863," in *Abraham Lincoln: Great Speeches* (New York: Dover Publications, 1991), 104.

[3] The Constitution of the United States, available at <www.archives.gov/exhibits/charters/constitution.html>.

[4] General Martin E. Dempsey, "Letter to the Joint Force," October 1, 2011, available at <www.dodlive.mil/index.php/2011/10/general-dempseys-letter-to-the-joint-force/>.

[5] The first three elements are borrowed from Samuel P. Huntington, *The Soldier and the State: The Theory and Politics of Civil-Military Relations* (Cambridge: Belknap Press of Harvard University Press, 1985), 8–18.

[6] Oaths of Enlistment and Oaths of Office, available at <www.history.army.mil/html/faq/oaths.html>.

[7] William Gainey, "SEAC Visits Goodfellow," *Air Force Print News Today*, July 2007, available at <www.goodfellow.af.mil/news/story_print.asp?id=123063260>.

[8] Kenneth O. Preston, "We Are Professionals," *The NCO Journal*, February 2011, 4.

Aneshea Yee

Marine Staff Sergeant Shakisha Traynham, Platoon 4032, Oscar Company, 4th Recruit Training Battalion, Recruit Training Regiment, Marine Corps Recruit Depot, Parris Island, Eastern Recruiting Region, looks left to right to make sure there are no corrections that need to be made before continuing on to the next drill movement during initial drill, August 29, 2011, aboard Marine Corps Recruit Depot Parris Island

CHAPTER THREE

Steward of the Institution

The scene is a grand ballroom. All eyes are glued to the center stage where a cake, on a cart, is marched forward between two columns of sword-carrying honor guards. The cake is beautifully decorated. Those in attendance are in their most ceremonial uniforms. Around the cake is a diverse mix of personnel, young and old, junior and senior. A Marine produces a sword from the cart and uses it to slice the elegant cake. The first piece is presented to the guest of honor. He takes a bite and smiles in appreciation. As the next piece is sliced off with the sword, the narrator announces, "The next piece is presented to the oldest Marine present. . . . Tonight the oldest Marine is Master Gunnery Sergeant Johnson. Master Gunnery Sergeant Johnson was born 48 years ago in Philadelphia, Pennsylvania. He enlisted in the Marine Corps 30 years ago and is currently assigned to Headquarters Marine Corps." The oldest Marine present then passes his piece of cake to the youngest Marine present. The narrator continues, "The passing of the cake from the oldest Marine to the youngest Marine symbolizes the passing of history and traditions from one generation to the next. . . . The youngest Marine present tonight is Private Jones. She was born 19 years ago in San Diego, California. She enlisted in the Marine Corps one year ago and is currently assigned to Headquarters Marine Corps."

The U.S. Marine Corps birthday cake–cutting ceremony represents a larger, deeper sense of unity and purpose inherent in the Profession of Arms, which spans generations. It also exemplifies a lineage of service to the Nation that embodies the unique culture and identity of the Corps. Additionally, it draws on the ethos of the Profession of Arms, which instills in its members a sense of pride and camaraderie, and inspires them to undertake endeavors that may require the "last full measure of devotion,"[1] which President Lincoln saluted in his Gettysburg Address.

The entrusting of history, customs, traditions, and standards by one generation to the next is a sacred duty. The institutions of the Armed Forces are given to the current generation by the proud warriors who came before. But these institutions do not belong to any one generation. The hallowed traditions of each Service branch belong to all the generations that came before, those who serve now, and those who will follow. The present generation simply preserves these treasures in trust for the future members of the force. This makes each and every member of the Armed Forces a *steward of the institution*. A steward is a guardian, a caretaker. Stewardship refers to a responsibility to take care of and improve something one does not own. In medieval times, a steward cared for a lord's household. In the end, the household is not the steward's to keep. The steward is expected to return the household in as good or better a condition than when he received it.

Joining the Armed Forces is a significant event for every young adult who dons the uniform. New members are expected to learn the history and the way of life that define their respective Service branches. Traditions are a defining part of the Profession of Arms, and they transcend the life cycle and career of all military members, officer and enlisted. Some traditions are presented at the time of entry into the Armed Forces. Others are passed on and practiced later. As members progress in their careers, they will be exposed to more traditions that commemorate specific events, promotions to specific ranks, and professional milestones. For example, one of the most celebrated and significant events in the Navy and Coast Guard is the advancement to the chief petty officer ranks in which the "Chiefs' Mess" welcomes new chiefs through a series of tasks and challenges. When petty officers become chief petty officers, not only do their responsibilities and duties grow, but their uniforms and social networks change as well. As members of the Chiefs' Mess, they have significantly greater responsibility, as well as the support and counsel of all the senior enlisted members of the command. At this point, each chief selectee has traditionally received intense orientation and indoctrination into many proud and storied traditions of the sea, thereby carrying on continued leadership development and nurturing of the newest formation of chief petty officers.

Traditions

Each of the Services that comprise the Armed Forces contributes to the defense of the Nation, its values, and its way of life. While the sum of these Services together is greater than any of the parts, it is important to maintain the remarkable flavor of each unique, individual Service. *E pluribus unum* (Latin for "Out of many, one") was the unofficial motto of the United States until 1956.[2] This simple phrase captures the sense that America as a nation is derived from many sources and traditions. It is this unity out of diversity that makes the Nation great, and it is the same unity out of diversity that makes the U.S. military a powerful, unified, and effective all-volunteer force.

In these early decades of the 21st century, NCOs/POs are more likely than their predecessors to serve in joint and multinational organizations. They may even find that they are the senior enlisted representatives of their respective Service branches, and as such it is their responsibility to represent their Services' traditions and standards. In other words, individual histories, lineage, customs, and courtesies of each Service bring unique capabilities, strengths, and pride to the greatest and most rewarding profession in the United States. Joint assignments require developing an understanding and respect for differences while learning to exploit the unique strengths of each Service to accomplish the mission. The same consideration holds when working with foreign military services.

While forged in the fires of battle and cemented over time, the traditions of the Services continue to grow, as new traditions are born and added over time. Although one should never forget what came before, there are chapters yet to be written. Servicemembers will add their own stories to the history of the Armed Forces. The Marine Corps cake-cutting ceremony mentioned above was not formalized until 1952. It had been an informal tradition conducted in various formats for decades before that. Today the cake-cutting ceremony exists as a polished part of a formal sequence with many symbolic elements.

Ceremonies are one aspect of tradition. Indeed, they are an integral part of the Profession of Arms. Young enlisted Servicemembers may be genuinely surprised at the ceremonies and trappings of their first promotions, while veterans after long careers may feel humbled by the idea of formal retirement ceremonies. However, these events are not only for the members being honored; they belong to the institution or organization. They celebrate the life cycle of the Servicemember and the vital continuity of the story. Just as the cake is passed from veteran to novice in the cake-cutting ceremony, so is the mantle of responsibility and leadership passed to new leaders as they rise within the organization.

The retirement ceremony of senior noncommissioned officers and chief petty officers is a time to reinforce the reality that the Services they leave behind are as devoted to duty and honor as they were the day the retiree entered. They have done their part to preserve—and to advance—the honor of their Services. They have done their part to build on the proud traditions. This is a time to reflect on the state of the Service and the Nation. Retirees may justifiably feel proud that they have kept their honor. Their successors stand ready to assume responsibility, to stand the watch, to carry on a proud tradition within the Profession of Arms.

Customs and courtesies serve many functions for NCOs/POs. They practice these customs not simply because they enjoy the pageantry, but for deeper reasons. Repeating these traditions at prescribed times and in precise detail is the practice of discipline. One example is rendering honors to the colors at "Reveille" and "Retreat." As Servicemembers of units internalize these traditions, a bond grows with those who also hold these traditions dear and thus learn why it is necessary to preserve them. To preserve an idea, members must protect those who value the idea. Their fellow Servicemembers share with them a love and belief in these values, and these values build bonds that last. This is the heart of esprit de corps, or spirit of the unit, which is the sense of unity that leads warriors on the battlefield to believe that the lives of those around them are more important than their own. The Oath of Enlistment speaks of defending the Constitution against all enemies foreign and domestic[3] because the Constitution is the written manifestation of the values they cherish. Article I of The Code of Conduct states, "I am an American, fighting in the forces which guard my Country and our way of life. I am prepared to give my life in their defense."[4]

The wars in Iraq and Afghanistan in the first decades of the 21st century continued the long story of this nation and its men and women in uniform. Those who fought will join the rolls of honor with the great warriors of the previous centuries. From these battles, and from the heroes who fought them, will spring new traditions and new chapters in the history of the Armed Forces.

Standards

Remember, too, that the company which takes pride in the snap and accuracy with which it does things on the parade ground is also most likely to be the company that will conform strictly to the requirements of discipline in garrison and in the field.

—Noncommissioned Officers' Manual, 1917[5]

As members of the Profession of Arms, all Servicemembers are stewards of the profession and its unique body of knowledge, the individual and collective commitment to service, and the obligation to maintain the integrity that defines the profession. Noncommissioned officers and petty officers do not simply ensure the continuity of this knowledge. They also advance the art and science of the Profession of Arms by expanding that knowledge, especially about the ultimate activity of a military—waging war. The ancient military philosopher Sun Tzu said of war: "It is a matter of life and death, a road to safety or ruin. Therefore, it is a subject that must be thoroughly studied."[6] The security of the American people, and the protection of their values and their way of life, demands that the Armed Forces aspire to the highest levels of professionalism.

As in every societal profession, there are those who are appointed to ensure that their members have the required knowledge to meet the established standard. Unique to the Profession of Arms, all NCOs/POs are traditionally charged as the torch bearers who maintain and enforce its standard. They are teachers, coaches, and mentors who pass on that knowledge. By learning to inspect and correct the imperfections in their subordinates, young enlisted leaders become accustomed to giving orders and holding their subordinates accountable. Those subordinates in turn become accustomed to following orders and looking for guidance from their mentors. If NCOs/POs deviate from standards, surely their subordinates will follow. Rather, NCOs/POs must embody the standards they wish to enforce, and thus become living examples. This is what is meant by *leading by example.*

There are many ways that NCOs/POs set the example for subordinates to follow. One is the wearing of their uniforms. NCOs/POs take pride in their appearance. Their uniform is the physical embodiment of their esprit de corps. The uniform regulations of the Navy, for instance, point out that "uniforms are distinctive visual evidence of the authority and responsibility vested in their wearer by the United States."[7] The uniform worn by Servicemembers communicates at least three things to an observer: the branch of Service to which they belong, the rank or grade to which they have been appointed, and the name of the wearer. But the smartness of the uniform is also an indicator to the observer of the discipline and pride of the men and women who wear it. Throughout history, units that are effective on the battlefield have also excelled at maintaining discipline in matters of uniforms, grooming, and personal appearance. NCOs/POs ensure that their own uniforms are beyond reproach, leading by example, and thus they are able to positively demand the same of the personnel they lead.

Another longstanding tradition in the Armed Forces of the United States is the salute. The origins of saluting are unknown. It may be that the tradition goes all the way back to ancient Rome where it was customary to show an open hand before approaching a public official. Medieval knights would raise their visors when greeting a friendly comrade. The practice of the salute is a sign of respect. In modern times, the hand salute is one of the most visible and important military courtesies, common to all Service branches.

One of the most important duties of an enlisted leader is to inspect personnel and to enforce standards. Once NCOs/POs have shown by personal example what they expect out of their subordinates, it is equally important to inspect those personnel to ensure that the example is followed. In combat, inspecting subordinates is a life or death business. By ensuring that the members of a unit have all of the equipment required for the mission—and that it is in good working order—NCOs/POs ensure the effectiveness of the unit and enhance the safety of its members. This attention to the needs of their teams strengthens the bond among them all. As esprit de corps grows, so does the morale of the unit, and in turn so does its effectiveness. The desire to accomplish the missions that NCOs/POs have been given—and to succeed in the tasks they have trained so hard for—becomes a powerful force.

The duty of all enlisted men and women is to observe and follow the example set by their leaders. Great leaders live the standards they enforce. So in that leader, subordinates have a living model for how to lead, support organizational goals, and enhance their professional and personal lives.

Responsibility to the Unit

The foundation and driving force of the Profession of Arms are its leaders. They provide an incalculable competitive advantage against our adversaries. They are the builders and maintainers of trust; they inspire others to achieve what they thought was beyond reach; they teach and mentor their subordinates to develop experts; and they uphold and enforce our ethical and moral standards regardless of the situation. . . . Today we have the finest officers and non-commissioned officers on the planet.[8]

—General Martin E. Dempsey

Noncommissioned officers and petty officers are the caretakers of their units. They are especially responsible for sustaining what is known as the command or organizational climate. Command climate encompasses esprit de corps, that is to say, how the members feel about their unit. The leaders of the unit nurture it through inspiration, personal example, and on-the-spot correction. Command or organization climate includes the members' perceptions of the commander, senior enlisted, others in the chain of command, and unit policies. A positive command climate yields the trust, pride, commitment, and unity that enable positive action and the ability to deal with uncertainty and change. Conversely, a negative or degraded command climate hinders productivity, and it generates mistrust, frustration, low motivation, and fragmentation. A negative command climate too often results in the emergence of informal leaders who may be influential but are not aligned with organizational goals. These disruptive voices may undercut the effectiveness of the appointed leadership and create additional morale and discipline issues. The NCO/PO is best positioned to anticipate these problems and best equipped to deal with them.

One role of the enlisted leader is to monitor the command climate. NCOs and POs know their people intimately; they know them as subordinates—but NCOs/POs also know how their subordinates feel about sports, current events, pop culture, and certainly the command. Enlisted leaders work constantly to shape, improve, maintain, and report the status of command climate. Enlisted leaders are the commander's eyes and ears. They are also the voice of the enlisted force to the commander. They regularly report on the state of morale, welfare, and discipline within the command. This is not just a litany of minor offenses. It requires context, experience, and judgment to inform the commander of indicators of low morale, such as spikes in discipline issues, or indicators of a high state of discipline, such as excellent appearance and proper maintenance of equipment and resources throughout the command. Commanders are not only looking for details. They are counting on enlisted leaders to employ critical thinking, provide judgment as to the degree of any potential problems, advise on how to rectify minor issues before they develop into problems, and recommend courses of action to keep the unit operating at its peak.

Command climate is also about how the members feel the command supports their needs. This is not only about food, mail, and pay, although those elements are important. Command climate refers specifically to commanders and the policies that they and the chain of command enact. While the role of commanders is central, in many ways enlisted leaders have much more influence over the command climate. It is also the duty of NCOs/POs to ensure that the members are receiving realistic and challenging training, which will prepare them for success in their assigned missions. NCOs/POs show that they care for the members of the command by holding them to the standard. They show that they care enough to inspect them and correct any deficiencies they find. This kind of professionalism is a consistent reminder to all the members that they are part of a proud organization. They can be confident of the men and women around them in the most perilous missions.

Even when command climate is good and things are going well, a significant event can challenge and affect the members of the unit. For example, unprofessional relationships may form within a command. They may take the form of fraternization, which might seem innocent enough as seniors and subordinates grow closer together, but that could result in roles becoming confused and discipline breaking down. It could also take the form of harassment or discrimination, which can produce a negative atmosphere within the command. If Servicemembers are the victims of racism or sexual harassment, for instance, and they believe the chain of command is not supporting them, they could lose faith in the chain of command. It is the duty of every NCO/PO to be constantly on the watch for these kinds of toxic situations, which must be addressed and corrected as promptly and effectively as possible.

Enlisted leaders care for the well-being of their personnel, which includes caring about their families. The service and sacrifice of military families are vital to the success of any unit. NCOs/POs are mindful that while the military members make tremendous sacrifices to serve the Nation, they can do so only with the support of their families. Frequent and extended separations due to deployments and duty create immense stress within families. In light of this reality, NCOs/POs play critical roles in ensuring that families are meaningfully supported and that quality support systems are in place during the absence of their military members. By doing so, NCOs/POs ensure that members can maintain their operational focus while remaining confident that their families will be fully taken care of. Families should find comfort in knowing that they too are contributing to a larger cause and are an integral part of the organization. NCOs/POs stay aware of potential home, personal, or financial problems that will distract from the mission. As the Senior Enlisted Advisor to the Chairman has pointed out, to maintain effectiveness while ensuring the welfare of the force and families, enlisted leaders must get better at "problem-*preventing*" rather than our normal reactive mode of "problem-*solving*."[9] At times it may be necessary to ensure that personnel have time or guidance in order to take care of financial or medical issues within the family. This kind of personal investment by NCOs/POs sends a clear message to the members and their families that *all of them* are important.

NCOs/POs also nurture good command climate through effective communication within the unit. They must make sure subordinates understand how to forward productive suggestions up the chain of command and how to address legitimate grievances. Modeling how to provide productive feedback is another way NCOs/POs can lead by example. They may advise their superiors in private, always respecting the superior's authority to decide and responsibility for outcomes. At the same time, they are unfailingly supportive and loyal in public and never undercut the chain of command, tolerate counterproductive speech and actions, or accept attitudes that degrade esprit de corps. If someone from outside the command is speaking disparagingly, the NCO/PO does not tolerate any kind of unprofessional degradation of his unit. On the other hand, losing trust and confidence that the chain of command will do the right thing can poison a command climate.

Noncommissioned officers/petty officers are the caretakers and stewards of the sacred traditions and history of the Armed Forces of the United States. These traditions have been forged in the fire of battles and honed by constant practice. Every generation of enlisted leaders has accepted the added weight of this charge and is worthy of it—and these leaders too will leave their Services and their professions better than they found them.

Notes

[1] Abraham Lincoln, "Address Delivered at the Dedication of the Cemetery at Gettysburg, 19 November 1863," in *Abraham Lincoln: Great Speeches* (New York: Dover Publications, 1991), 104.

[2] The United States of America did not have an official motto until 1956. "In God We Trust" was adopted as the official motto, although many still consider "*E pluribus unum*" to be a second, unofficial motto. See John D. MacArthur, "Latin Mottoes," *GreatSeal.com*, available at <www.greatseal.com/mottoes/unum.html>.

[3] Title 10 U.S. Code, Subtitle A—General Military Law, Part II—Personnel, Chapter 31—Enlistments.

⁴ Executive Order 10631—Code of Conduct for members of the Armed Forces of the United States, August 17, 1955, available at <www.archives.gov/federal-register/codification/executive-order/10631.html>.

⁵ James A. Moss, *Noncommissioned Officers' Manual* (Washington, DC: U.S. Infantry Association, 1917), 17.

⁶ R.L. Cantrell, *Sun Tzu on the Art of War* (Arlington, VA: Center for Advantage, 2003), 76.

⁷ Navy Personnel Command, "United States Navy Uniform Regulations," available at <www.public.navy.mil/bupers-npc/support/uniforms/uniformregulations/Pages/default.aspx>.

⁸ Martin E. Dempsey, "America's Military—A Profession of Arms," 4–5, available at <www.jcs.mil/content/files/2012-02/022312120752_Americas_Military_POA.pdf>.

⁹ Bryan B. Battaglia, "Bridging the Basics," *Joint Force Quarterly* 68 (1ˢᵗ Quarter 2013), 6–7.

Chief Petty Officer Kent Shafer of the U.S. Coast Guard Academy and Lieutenant Kristopher Ensley, operations officer aboard Coast Guard Barque Eagle, *discuss the* Eagle*'s approach into Greenport, New York, September 20, 2012. The* Eagle *is the Coast Guard's training platform for future officers*

CHAPTER FOUR

Complementing the Officer

From the first moment of contact with the commander and other commissioned officers, noncommissioned officers/petty officers have the opportunity to show their abilities and determination to support and enforce the goals of the unit and to demonstrate effective leadership of the enlisted force. By doing so over time, NCOs/POs gain the trust of all the officers in the unit. One key competency for success in this critical role is the ability of the noncommissioned officer/petty officer to understand, pass on, and explain the *commander's intent*—that is, "the commander's clear and concise expression of what the force must do and the conditions the force must establish to accomplish the mission."[1] The ability of the NCO/PO to understand the commander's intent, coupled with earned trust to execute it, is the foundation of the officer-NCO/PO relationship. This understanding greatly contributes to unity of command, ensures continuity of mission, and instills confidence that orders will be carried out promptly and effectively. The overall benefit from this method of operating is no disruption or loss of momentum to the mission in the absence of the commissioned leader. NCOs/POs make sure that the endstate will be reached in the face of whatever contingencies arise. This well-defined and well-understood relationship reinforces unit integrity, discipline, and overall mission accomplishment.

A positive and professional relationship between the two leaders creates and sustains healthy and productive organizational/command climate. These roles and responsibilities come with expectations of performance and sacrifice. Developing a positive and professional relationship between the enlisted leader and commissioned officer requires diligence and frequent self-assessment. NCOs/POs who enjoy a close relationship with their officers find it one of the most satisfying parts of their service. It does not, however, privilege NCOs/POs beyond their station or position in the organization. It is important for NCOs/POs to remain grounded in supporting the unit's mission by complementing their officers and enabling the force. NCOs/POs must remember that performing the dual roles is not about them; it is about the men and women they support and lead. In the more senior NCO/PO ranks, a considerable amount of leeway is afforded to enlisted leaders and advisors because of the stringent selection process and their time in service, expertise, and experience.

There is but one commander of any given unit or organization. That officer, whether a lieutenant/ensign or a general/admiral, is in command. That officer's corresponding NCO/PO is a principal advisor, a source of competence and counsel, who enhances the officer's ability to command effectively. If NCOs/POs understand this time-tested concept and direct their efforts to those things that the commander needs them to focus on and to those matters they realize require their attention, they serve as force multipliers. This can be described as the *art* of the officer-NCO/PO relationship. NCOs/POs bring distinctive perspective and experience. They can assist with critical thinking, development of courses of action, implementation of decisions or change, and perhaps most importantly, they add the voice of the enlisted personnel to the discussion of issues facing the chain of command. NCOs/POs can forfeit the trusted advisor role quickly if they do not bring professionalism, maturity, and competence to the equation, or if they lose the proper perspective of that unique role. They must never appear to supersede the official chain of command or impede the force from accomplishing what needs to be done based on orders or guidance from the commander.

The Oath of Enlistment clearly defines the relationship with officers: "obey the orders of the President of the United States and the orders of the officers appointed over me." Even in this new century, with a mature all-volunteer force and substantially higher degrees of responsibility and empowerment of NCOs/POs, it must be clearly understood that the words of that oath are sacred, enduring, and binding. As much as some NCOs/POs prefer to use phrases such as *my unit* and *my decision*, the reality is that it is *our unit* and *the commander's decision.* Commanders can—and often will—take into consideration the recommendations of enlisted leaders as they are making the final decision, but the responsibility to decide, and the expectation of loyal obedience, remains with the commander.

In military units, newly commissioned officers, regardless of Service, will benefit greatly from the advice and support of seasoned enlisted leaders who will help guide them in their role as the officer-in-charge or the commander of the platoon, flight, or section. Newly commissioned lieutenants or ensigns will become savvier over time, and through their own experience they will gain a more refined and informed perspective. That professional development and maturation can be shaped positively by the right NCOs/POs, who can have lasting, positive effects on those officers. At times, junior personnel may look at senior officers and wonder why they utilize their enlisted leaders in a certain way. Many times an officer's desire to empower an enlisted leader, or to minimize that enlisted leader's role, is a reflection of that officer's initial exposure to enlisted leadership. Officers will indeed weigh and measure NCOs/POs based largely on their exposure to NCOs/POs throughout their careers, but perhaps especially on their earliest relationships and experiences with NCOs/POs. The continued viability of the NCO/PO role depends to a significant degree on this first officer-NCO/PO relationship.

Newly commissioned officers usually come to the fleet, company, or squadron with an undergraduate degree but little military experience. Often the enlisted leaders in those units will have less formal education, but they bring a wealth of experience and technical competence that compensate for variances in education and narrow the gap between them and their new officers. Because of their increased complexity, the evolving roles and expectations of NCOs/POs in the 21st century will require increasing their civilian and professional education levels without disturbing proven organizational integrity or diluting the status of either officers or enlisted personnel.

To be successful in building and sustaining this kind of relationship with officers, NCOs/POs must be *competent*, *credible*, and *capable*.

Competent: NCOs/POs are competent both in their specific skill sets or occupational specialties/rates and in the "tribal knowledge" of the units and what makes them tick. They have to be technically and tactically proficient, better than their subordinates and ready to assume the next higher billet. Through their practical knowledge and ability to apply it to any given situation, they complement their officers and enhance both their own and the officers' performance. Taking the time to explain—and backing up the explanation with more than "that is the way it has always been done"—will add to the relationship and will be instrumental in the maturation of the officers with whom NCOs/POs serve. Through actions more than words, the enlisted-officer relationship will grow, and that growth will become the foundation for a powerful team.

Credible: Credibility—being worthy of belief or confidence—must be built over time and is extremely difficult to recover if lost. Especially in times of uncertainty, the credibility of the NCO/PO will weigh heavily in the officer's decisionmaking. As with any leader, when NCOs/POs join a military unit, parts of their careers or portfolios follow them from previous assignments. It is during this early assessment that their reputations and credibility are accepted—or not. This is likely the baseline from which they build or lose credibility within the command. Providing relevant recommendations will become natural with preparation and practice. Knowing the strengths and weaknesses of the unit, and studying the mission and its people while understanding the commander's intent, are essential in that preparation and will assist in gaining credibility.

Regardless of the specific issues that may arise within the organization, a strong and productive officer-NCO/PO relationship based on trust will always contribute to success. Building and nurturing trust in this relationship are essential to good order and discipline, and *trust is the foundation of unit effectiveness.* What can be given can also be lost or taken away, so once that trust is afforded, it must be safeguarded. If that trust is ever lost due to inappropriate action, or lack of action, it is difficult to regain. The credibility of NCOs/POs is tied to the trust reposed in them. It starts with the officer trusting the NCO/PO to accomplish the mission without direct or constant supervision. The credibility of NCOs/POs grows in the eyes of officers when those individuals demonstrate that they are trustworthy. As credibility grows over time, so does trust. This only underscores an idea in a preceding paragraph: actions will speak louder than words.

Capable: Some NCOs/POs are competent, and some are credible, but what brings certain NCOs/POs to the forefront is that they are *capable*; that is, they are able to *apply* their expert knowledge (competence) to real tasks in the real world. Being able to teach tactics in a sterile environment is one thing, but can those same NCOs/POs execute those tactics when taking enemy fire? Are they capable of taking the information and applying it under conditions of stress and confusion? *Capable* NCOs/POs can perform at will, unsupervised, and produce desired results. More often than not, the capability the NCO/PO brings to the equation will be the difference between mission accomplishment and substandard results. When the NCO/PO possesses a known capability that can be directed toward a problem, that capability is a force multiplier for both the commander and the unit. Much like a good blade, it must be sharpened frequently to maintain relevancy. When used but not sharpened, it becomes dull and less useful. The most capable NCOs/POs work continually to improve their capabilities, and they become increasingly useful, indeed invaluable, to their officers, personnel, and families.

Competent, credible, and capable are the three Cs, used here to illustrate a well-rounded formula for enlisted leaders to execute their duties effectively. But *attitude* and *approachability* also play a significant role in the officer-NCO/PO relationship. It is said that "amateurs advertise." The officers above the NCOs/POs, and the subordinates below them, will take notice and respond positively to quality leadership and a strong presence, but not to bragging or self-promotion. A good officer-NCO/PO relationship benefits from humility. If NCOs/POs are well versed in the Profession of Arms *and* have humility, their contribution to the officer-enlisted relationship will positively reflect throughout the command. If NCOs/POs aim for personal glory or accolades, everyone around them will see it. Broadcasting one's self-image weakens leadership; it poisons the command climate. Officers appreciate humility in their NCOs/POs and value the ones who allow their abilities to speak instead of themselves. Being humble and getting the mission done without seeking personal recognition is a testament to the NCO/PO commitment to the Profession of Arms. This display of selfless and humble performance will endear them to the officer and will build trust and confidence in their relationship.

Being approachable is also key when dealing with officers, subordinates, and peers. NCOs/POs can be competent, credible, and capable yet still not be approachable. Approachable enlisted leaders encourage new officers to reach out to them to get their perspectives on issues. Unapproachable enlisted leaders have the opposite effect and may either unintentionally or intentionally discourage a productive officer-NCO/PO relationship. Some may label it as "burning a bridge." If they have an approachable enlisted leader they can turn to, new lieutenants and ensigns will gain wisdom and grow in their professionalism. Being approachable is not a sign of weakness, but rather a sign of confidence and strength. Being approachable will facilitate synergy and help the NCO/PO guide the officer's decisions, thus enhancing unit cohesion and effectiveness.

The commander and the enlisted leader have an obligation to be a moral backstop for all members of the organization. Specifically, the manner in which NCOs/POs behave in both their professional and their personal lives will set an example for all who observe them. This involves more than lip service to a policy or regulation. It encompasses the enlisted leader's whole persona and will become infectious in the organization. Doing what is right—and not what is convenient—is a hard road to travel, but it will pay considerable dividends when ethical dilemmas confront leadership. Ethically sound NCOs/POs will become part of the conscience of the unit, and no one will want to let them down. In essence, the NCOs/POs can be the moral compass of the unit that will help keep it going in the right direction. It takes moral courage to set this example, but it is well worth the effort, and it will produce positive and lasting results for the entire force.

No man is an island and no leader—officer or enlisted—can expect or even hope to be effective, especially in moments of crisis and during trying times, without the support, faith, and confidence of others within the leadership team. The officer-NCO/PO relationship is a sacred feature in the Profession of Arms. It is built on mutual recognition of their respective roles and responsibilities, and a true appreciation of the contribution of each. An officer-NCO/PO relationship can be toxic, passive, or positive, but what each one brings to the table can have profound and far-reaching effects, from command climate to the overall capacity of the organization. While the relationship is a shared effort, NCOs/POs are at their best when they nurture it through example, perseverance, and persistence.

Note
   [1] Joint Publication 3-0, *Joint Operations* (Washington, DC: The Joint Staff, 2011).

Staff Sergeant John Wheeler teaches Corporal Cody Kapotak specifics about his military occupation in Helmand Province, Afghanistan, August 12, 2011. SSgt Wheeler is communications maintenance chief, communications platoon sergeant, electronic warfare officer, and the Marine Corps Martial Arts Program instructor trainer for 1ˢᵗ Battalion, 3ʳᵈ Marine Regiment (1/3). This deployment is his first time to Afghanistan, but his third deployment. Cpl Kapotak is communications maintenance noncommissioned officer for 1/3.

CHAPTER FIVE

Enabling the Force

Enabling the force is one of the most important functions and responsibilities of noncommissioned officers/petty officers. All noncommissioned officers/petty officers are responsible and accountable for their own development, but most importantly they are responsible for the development of their subordinates. They contribute to the development of their peers collaterally, and in many important ways they contribute to the development of the officers with whom they serve. As Chief Master Sergeant Denise M. Jelinski-Hall, USAF, former Senior Enlisted Advisor for the National Guard Bureau, noted, the effort is well worth it: "Investing daily in . . . personal growth will yield extraordinary success." From using creative and critical thinking to identify needs and courses of action to teaching "how we do something" and "why we do something," NCOs/POs are the key players in the development, advancement, and sustainment of the force.

Leadership, regardless of level or status, involves managing tasks and relationships. NCOs/POs take the lead in helping their junior enlisted members focus on the task at hand, perform their duties to the best of their abilities, and develop productive relationships with the other members of the organization. NCOs/POs must understand themselves, their peers, their superiors, and most importantly the people they lead if they are to develop their subordinates into better followers and, ultimately, effective leaders.

Great leaders understand the importance of developing and maintaining professional relationships. These relationships allow leaders to understand the wants and needs of their followers and to ensure that the members of the force are properly cared for at work and at home. This attention promotes a resilient force capable of dealing with adversity. The bottom line is that leaders take care of their people so their people can take care of the mission.

The U.S. Armed Forces are developed from within. Senior leaders are not hired from outside the organization; they rise from within their Services over entire careers. Therefore, it is incumbent upon leaders to develop subordinates who will one day be the successors to the very leaders who trained them. To this end, NCOs/POs develop their subordinates through teaching, coaching, and mentoring.

Teaching

Teaching—the imparting of information and knowledge—is a primary function for enlisted leaders. They are the teachers, and their subordinates are their students. In this relationship, NCOs/POs possess the necessary information and knowledge their subordinates need to succeed. They ensure that their subordinates possess the requisite knowledge for the day-to-day operations of the command or unit. This involves more than just teaching the technical aspects of their jobs. NCOs/POs ensure that their subordinates are properly developed in all aspects of their lives in order to accomplish their missions. Basic life skills such as individual and family financial planning and management, and mental and physical preparedness, all contribute to the mission readiness of individual Servicemembers.

The most essential subject matter that NCOs/POs teach is the *science* of the Profession of Arms—the basics, the nuts and bolts of military skills and competencies. Developing and honing proficiency in individual military skills and specialty expertise represent the sweet spot of NCO/PO roles and responsibilities.

Coaching

While teaching imparts information and knowledge, coaching focuses on developing and refining skills. Coaching involves overseeing the repetitive practice of skills until they are mastered. A key component of coaching is leaders' praise and constructive criticism of their subordinates. Coaching involves the determined effort to help subordinates develop the desire and capacity to achieve professional and personal goals. Subordinates must be motivated, and NCOs/POs provide the inspiration. Enlisted leaders are role models for their subordinates. Forbidden in the teachings of any military leadership guide is the slogan, "Do as I say, not as I do." Rather, the enlisted leader leads by example. Said in simpler form, *NCOs/POs live a life ready for inspection.*

NCOs/POs develop specific job-related competencies for their subordinates and work with them to clarify and refine their short- and long-term career and life goals. Helping subordinates develop strategies to deal with difficult people, and to manage difficult emotions in the workplace, is critical. Coaches provide feedback and encouragement. The endstate is learning, competence, and confidence.

The adage "watch one, do one, teach one" is paramount. Coaching is collaborative: leaders impart the required information and knowledge and then allow their subordinates to demonstrate their mastery of it, offering positive correction where it is required. NCOs/POs also empower their subordinates to become the coaches for the next generation.

In contrast to teaching, coaching involves a balanced mix of the art and science of the Profession of Arms. Only when Servicemembers have acquired the basic skills are they ready to begin to absorb the *art* of the profession.

Mentoring

Teaching imparts new knowledge, and coaching develops and refines new skills, but mentoring is the apex of subordinate development. While there is some science involved, mentoring takes both the mentor and protégé deeply into the art of leadership and the Profession of Arms. This is where wisdom enters the picture. Mentoring by more experienced professionals enables subordinates to tap into their own talents, traits, and resources in order to mature and develop not only as military professionals but also as human beings. A mentor-protégé relationship is complex, and it contains elements of both teaching and coaching. While mentors may be assigned, the best mentors are chosen—chosen by their subordinates because they embody the attributes and qualities to emulate. Mentors are often outside the formal chain of command, selected because of their reputation or observed performance. Subordinates often seek out mentors who share common interests or values. As a mentor, an NCO/PO enhances a subordinate's knowledge and mastery of the job—and of life.

The NCO/PO mentor commits to the subordinate and vice versa because both are looking for a sustained professional relationship that will serve a higher purpose. For the NCO/PO, mentorship provides an opportunity to influence and develop the full potential of others. NCOs/POs draw on their wisdom and inherent knowledge—and those of their subordinates—to allow the rising generation to develop and flourish. More than skill acquisition and knowledge transfer, mentoring involves cultivating the whole person—values, passions, and goals. A mentor provides guidance and direction on setting and achieving goals and helps subordinates become more deeply steeped in Service cultures. The endstate is for subordinates to take on the essence of the Service ethos—the culture, philosophy, and way of life. Subordinates who are properly mentored are more committed not only to their careers, but also to their commands, their Services, and the Armed Forces. Everyone benefits from a good mentoring relationship.

Critical Thinking

One important aspect of professional and personal development is nurturing critical thinking, which involves developing and maintaining an analytical attitude. Responding to life-and-death situations—flooding on a ship, an aircraft emergency, or a firefight—calls primarily for reactive thinking, drawing on training and experience to make a sound split-second decision. In contrast, critical thinking is a more deliberate contemplation of decisions and anticipation of possible courses of action, and accordingly it yields better understanding and stimulates creativity. Critical thinking is a process by which leaders, as well as subordinates, evaluate decisions and actions to answer relevant tough questions and challenge assumptions.

Practicing critical thinking enables leaders to react more quickly, decisively, and effectively in moments of crisis or combat. As critical thinkers, NCOs/POs are adept at evaluating how they see the world. Accepting the status quo as a permanent condition ensures that the force will become stagnant. NCOs/POs challenge a specific method of operating and then evaluate it critically with an eye toward greater efficiency and effectiveness. Critical thinking is perhaps most needed when someone says, "We've always done it this way." This is when asking "*Why?*" is paramount; this is the time to evaluate whether the way of doing something is still practical and relevant. It then falls to experienced and wise NCOs/POs to make sound recommendations to their chains of command to ensure that the organization and force are always improving.

Enlisted leaders prepare themselves and their subordinates for the unknown. While training hones the ability to perform, education broadens intellectual capacity. Both training and education enhance the ability to anticipate and react to the unknown. The U.S. military owes its success to a long history of developing its people for the unknown. Not long ago, no one would have thought an attack over the Internet could cripple a nation. However, great thinkers—critical thinkers—anticipated this threat and initiated training and education programs that have enabled today's Armed Forces to protect both space and cyber domains. As experienced and empowered leaders, NCOs/POs evaluate situations critically and understand the environments in which they operate. Then they ensure that they and their subordinates are trained, educated, and prepared to deal with unanticipated situations and scenarios.

Empowerment

People are empowered when they are encouraged to think, behave, decide, and act on their own. This empowerment does not spring up spontaneously. Rather, it must be fostered and instilled by leaders. Only when that is done do individuals come to feel genuinely empowered. This sense allows them to grow in self-confidence through a process of continuous self-development to remain relevant and sharp. With empowerment comes a higher form of accountability. In the Profession of Arms, power and accountability are inextricably linked: the more power and responsibility individuals have, the more they are held accountable. NCOs/POs are champions for empowerment within their commands. They ensure that subordinates not only understand and fully trust in this empowerment, but that they also put it to good use for the benefit of the organization or unit.

Self-development comes in many forms, and failure is one. Traditionally, failure is looked on as calling for punishment. In an environment of true empowerment, though, failure becomes an avenue for self-development, with minimal outside corrective action and rarely with punishment. Empowerment transforms shortfalls or mistakes from an occasion for punishment into an opportunity to learn. Therefore, NCOs/POs must adequately communicate this process to their subordinates. Failure through malice, negligence, or gross incompetence is not self-development and not part of the empowerment process, but failure through understandable human error, used reflectively and self-critically for learning, can be—and should be—part of the empowerment process.

It is up to NCOs/POs to fully understand their subordinates and their abilities, weaknesses, and willingness to take risks. This allows NCOs/POs to assign tasks and actions commensurate with their subordinates' abilities. Ultimately they are training their replacements, so they must ensure that additional opportunities open up for continuing the development process.

Force Development

Professional and personal development of subordinates requires a balance of specialized training (qualification, certification, and readiness) and professional education (expanding intellectual capacity) to round out a member of the Profession of Arms. The complex and rapidly changing environment of the 21st century calls for renewed attention to both training and education for the enlisted force. NCOs/POs are taking the lead in rethinking what is required for tomorrow's military.

As stewards of the institution, NCOs/POs understand that professional development involves more than training that leads to certification and qualification and education that leads to expanded intellectual capacity. It also includes the development of mental and physical readiness. The Profession of Arms depends on NCOs/POs to be exemplary role models, specialized experts, thoughtful counselors, competent career and life-skills advisors, and approachable coaches and mentors. NCOs/POs invest in their people, and by doing so, they yield a better professional and a better citizen. They encourage personal growth through advocacy of off-duty education, realizing that a more educated subordinate is more likely to be a more effective leader. They lead and motivate their subordinates to meet and exceed physical standards because they know that physical fitness supports endurance and resilience. They challenge subordinates mentally because they know that doing so will result in a critically thinking warrior who can endure the stress and uncertainty of combat or crisis.

NCOs/POs embody and impart unyielding moral standards and values. They are responsible for what they do—and for what they fail to do—and for developing subordinates to do the same through teaching, coaching, and mentoring. As Chief Master Sergeant of the Air Force James Roy stated, "The fundamental building block of leadership is establishing, communicating, and maintaining clear standards. NCOs are entrusted with the awesome responsibility of preparing young Servicemembers to meet joint force mission requirements." They are guided by the importance of mission accomplishment and their responsibility to develop future leaders—leaders who will assume their place and continue to enable the force.

Joint Service Color Guard advances colors during retirement ceremony of Chairman of the Joint Chiefs of Staff General Henry H. Shelton, Fort Myer, Virginia, October 2, 2001

CHAPTER SIX

Service Identity and Joint Warfighting

[Note: This chapter was first published as chapter 8, "Service Identity and Joint Warfighting," in The Armed Forces Officer *(NDU Press and Potomac Books, 2007). The original version has been modified here.]*

The days of any Service (Active duty or Reserve component) operating as a truly independent actor are gone. The five Services fight together as a team, which means they must plan and train as a team. This in turn means that, in order to be effective leaders, 21st-century noncommissioned officers/petty officers must know something about the other Services.

Fighting, living, or operating as a joint force does not mean that all Services play equal parts in every battle or exercise. It does mean that they are partners in the overall business of defending the United States, its territory, population, and national interests, and therefore the best each has to offer must be woven into every plan, exercise, and battle. There can be no "lone wolves" among the Services because U.S. security cannot afford such free agency. When the Nation is threatened, the Navy does not go to war, nor does the Army; the Nation goes to war, using all of the Services' capabilities in the combination that best suits the particular threat posed and the war plan designed to defeat it.

While "jointness" has become the shorthand description for this five-Service partnership (with its own color, purple), there is another way to characterize the relationship among them, one with deep roots in American history and political culture: *E pluribus unum*—from many, one. Inscribed on the banner held in the beak of the eagle on the Great Seal of the United States, approved by Congress on June 20, 1782, these words convey the reality that out of the original 13 colonies, one nation emerged.[1] The 13 new states kept their own identities, but together they constituted one nation that was not just the sum of the 13, but greater than the total when combined.

So, too, from five Service branches comes the one entity charged with the defense of the Nation—the Armed Forces of the United States. Tradition and identity, including uniforms and customs, matter. So do the requirements generated by the distinctive roles the various Services perform in fighting on land, at sea, in the air, and in space, and the different capabilities they bring to the battle. Thus, the Services keep their separate traditions and identities, their distinctive uniforms and customs, but out of them emerges a single armed force that, because of the synergies among them, is greater, more flexible, and more capable than the mere sum.

This book is all about being an NCO or PO in the Armed Forces of the United States in the 21st century. This involves being a Soldier, Marine, Sailor, Airman, or Coastguardsman, each maintaining a distinctive identity, but it also involves being a member of something larger. Being a fully effective NCO or PO requires knowing one's own Service well (its capabilities as well as its limitations), and knowing the other Services well enough to appreciate their strengths and weaknesses, what they bring to the fight, and how their capabilities can best mesh.

On a deeper level, each Service has its own culture. It is culture that best defines and describes any organization. It also best defines and describes what it means to be a member of that organization. Thus, part of this chapter's contribution to understanding what it means to be an NCO or PO in the Armed Forces is to capture, albeit in snapshot style, the culture of each of the Services. As used here, *culture* is taken to have two meanings: at the organizational level, how this Service defines and sees itself, and at the individual level, what it means to be a Soldier, Marine, Sailor, Airman, or Coastguardsman.

Army

Army Service culture is founded on a fundamental belief in the *human dimension of war* and the *centrality of land combat* in its

I WANT YOU

for the U.S. ARMY
ENLIST NOW

prosecution. The Army sees its two core competencies as "[t]raining and equipping soldiers and growing leaders" and "[p]roviding relevant and ready land power to Combatant Commanders as part of the Joint Force."[2] It believes that its purpose, as part of the joint team, is to fight and win the Nation's wars. Since its founding during the American Revolution, the Army has operated in concert with allies and the other Services. The Army acknowledges the interdependence of all the Armed Forces, indeed their necessary operational integration, but Soldiers cannot imagine any military objective worth accomplishing that does not require dominance on land—"boots on the ground," to be decisive. Historian and veteran T.R. Fehrenbach wrote in his history of the Korean War: "[You] may fly over a land forever; you may bomb it, atomize it, pulverize it and wipe it clean of life—but if you desire to defend it, protect it, and keep it for civilization, you must do this on the ground, the way the Roman legions did, by putting your young men into the mud."[3]

Every Soldier a Warrior. The Army's unique function is found in Title 10, U.S. Code: "It shall be organized, trained, and equipped primarily for prompt and sustained combat incident to operations on land." The Army culture puts a high premium on the quality of individual and unit endurance.

The Army perceives its operational environment to be complex and challenging. Its ground forces are organized in a hierarchy of headquarters, each of which controls a number of subordinate units performing multiple coordinated tasks simultaneously. Command and control are fragile. The risk of surprise is omnipresent, and mobility advantage is often relatively limited vis-à-vis the adversary's. Land forces fight with multiple echelons from theater commander to squad leader, compared with two or three for sea or air forces.

The nature of land combat underscores a preference for organizational autonomy and redundancy, which tends to prejudice Soldiers against relying on others for essential ingredients of tactical survival and success. It also makes Army officers and NCOs instinctive planners who try to minimize chance by detailed study and anticipation.

America's Army. The Army identifies itself intimately with the Nation. Because it sees itself as a citizen force, it perceives itself to have a unique relationship with, as well as unique obligations to, the American people. Officers and NCOs alike are inculcated with a sense of obligation to ensure the Soldier's well-being that sometimes achieves a near parity with the obligation to accomplish assigned missions: "Mission First, People Always."

Soldiers value doctrine, theory, and history. The Soldier prefers troop duty to the staff, training to education, and the practical to the theoretical. At the same time, many NCOs read some theory, and there is always a subculture of thinkers ready to fill the pages of the Services' professional journals. Professional schools form a central part of the Army career for both commissioned and noncommissioned officers. Success in the Army is built on the cult of the commander, the one who gets things done, personally responsible for all that the unit does or fails to do. The NCO is an integral partner in that effort.

The Army Is People. The Army views itself as the most human-centered Service, yet it demands enormous human sacrifice. The Soldier is seen both as indomitable in battle and merciful to those in need, noncombatants and defeated foes alike. Consider General Order 100 from 1863: "Men who take up arms against one another in public war do not cease on this account to be moral beings responsible to one another."[4] The Army perceives itself to be an institution of values. At the core of the Army's self-identity is *The Soldier*. The Army asserts that it equips Soldiers; it does not man equipment.

Selfless service is a core value of the Army and of the Soldier: sacrifice for comrades, sacrifice for country, and if necessary, wounds and loss of life. The Tomb of the Unknowns is its most sacred monument. At Antietam, the Soldier Monument is marked with the phrase "Not for themselves but for their country."

Marine Corps

Marines are different. They have their own air arm, and they deploy on land and at sea. They have a hymn, not a song. Marines are different because of their ethos. Chapter 1 of Marine Corps Warfighting Publication 6-11, *Leading Marines*, is titled "Our Ethos." The introduction to that publication captures the essence of the Marine Corps ethos:

ANYONE CAN HEAR CHAOS. MARINES MOVE TO SILENCE IT.

MARINES.COM

Being a Marine comes from the eagle, globe, and anchor that is tattooed on the soul of every one of us who wears the Marine Corps uniform. . . . Unlike physical or psychological scars, which over time, tend to heal and fade in intensity, the eagle, globe, and anchor only grow more defined—more intense—the longer you are a Marine. "Once a Marine, always a Marine."[5]

That tattoo reflects a selfless spirit of being one of the few. Ask any Marine what he or she does, and the answer will be "I'm a Marine." What is most important to a Marine is *being* a Marine, not what rank or military occupational specialty he or she holds. It is the culture of the Marine Corps that makes it different not only from society as a whole, but also from the other Services. The Marine Corps is determined to be different—in military appearance, obedience to orders, disciplined behavior, adherence to traditions, and most important, the unyielding conviction that the Corps exists to fight. It has a deep appreciation for its rich history and traditions, which instills pride and responsibility in every Marine down to the lowest levels. Older Marines pass the traditions of the Corps to younger ones, ensuring they understand that the successes and sacrifices of the past set the path for the future. Since the first two battalions of Marines were raised by an act of the Continental Congress in 1775, many recruited from Tun Tavern in Philadelphia, the Corps has distinguished itself in every conflict in our nation's history. What follows are some of the more important characteristics that have shaped Marine Corps culture not only in the past, but also today.

Every Marine Is a Rifleman. In fact, *every* Marine, officer or enlisted, is trained first to be a rifleman before being trained in any other specialty. It is this bedrock premise and the training that goes with it that set all Marines on a common foundation. Leaders are molded with the same training given to those they will lead, building empathy and understanding unattainable in the other Services. Every facet of the Marine Corps exists to support the rifleman, and every Marine understands that.

Taking Care of Our Own. The characteristic that best defines Marines is *selflessness*—a spirit that places the self-interest of the individual after that of the institution and the team, all working toward a common goal. It is important that the unit succeed, *not* the individual. It is common to hear Marines speak of their leaders based on how well they take care of subordinates. "Take care of your people" and "take care of each other" are imbued in Marines from their first day in the Corps. Officers and NCOs eat last. They inspect the chow hall by eating in it. They know how their troops live in the barracks because they go there, and in the field they never have more creature comforts than their troops do. The only privilege of rank is that of ensuring that your subordinates are cared for. This culture defines what the Marine Corps is and who Marines are: men and women who exhibit extraordinary leadership and courage, both physical and moral, shaped by their dedication to the institution and each other.

Combined Arms Expeditionary Forces in Readiness. Operationally, there are four generally accepted characteristics that define and describe the Marine Corps. First, although capable of deploying and employing by various means, the Marine specialty is *amphibiousness*: the Corps comes from the sea, thus Marines think of themselves as "Soldiers of the Sea." Therefore, the Service focuses primarily on the coastal or littoral regions of the world. Second, the Marine Corps trains and operates as a *Marine Air-Ground Task Force*, a combined-arms, air-ground team, logistically self-sustainable for short periods of time. Third, as a *force-in-readiness*, the Marine Corps is a national "swing force"—forward deployed and expeditionary by nature—ready to respond rapidly to crises. Fourth, the Marine Corps considers itself a *light-to-medium force*, packing a quick and lethal punch. Although prepared to operate across the full spectrum of conflict, the Corps is more at home and most effective as a light-to-medium force that can be on scene quickly with enough firepower and sustainability to conduct operations as an "enabling force" until heavier units arrive.

The Marine Corps Is Small. As part of its expeditionary nature, the operating forces of the Marine Corps live on "camps," not forts or bases, and maintain a high tooth-to-tail ratio, relying on the other Services for a large portion of logistics, transportation, education, and combat service support. Many Marines receive specialized training at the other Service schools. There are no Marine doctors, nurses, dentists, field medical corpsmen, or chaplains—all of these are provided by the Navy. The Air Force and Navy get the Marines to the fight, with the Army assisting toward sustainment if Marines are forward deployed for extended periods.

Most Active-duty Marine forces are in the operating forces, with the bulk of those forces in the Fleet Marine Forces. These operating forces provide the combat power that is immediately available to the combatant commanders for employment.

To Marines, *expeditionary* means more than just getting there quickly. The Marines in the operating forces—most living in a Spartan-like "temporary-residence" mindset when not deployed—are eager members of the combined-arms team. This team is tailored toward a maneuver warfare approach to combat, where power from the sea is projected across the littoral, ideally maximizing the combined effect of its resources at a critical seam of the enemy's defense.

In 1957, the Commandant of the Marine Corps asked Lieutenant General Victor Krulak, "Why does the United States need a Marine Corps?" Five days later, General Krulak replied:

Essentially, as a result of the unfailing conduct of our Corps over the years, they (our nation's citizens) believe three things about Marines. First they believe when trouble comes to our country there will be Marines—somewhere—who, through hard work, have made and kept themselves ready to do something useful about it, and do it at once.

Second, they believe that when the Marines go to war they invariably turn in a performance that is dramatically and decisively successful—not most of the time, but always. Their faith and their convictions in this regard are almost mystical.

The third thing they believe about Marines is that our Corps is downright good for . . . our country; that the Marines are masters of a form of unfailing alchemy which converts unoriented youths into proud, self-reliant stable citizens—citizens into whose hands the nation's affairs may safely be entrusted.

Krulak concluded:

I believe the burden of all this can be summarized by saying that, while the functions which we discharge must always be done by someone, and while an organization such as ours is the correct one to do it, still, in terms of cold mechanical logic, the United States does not need a Marine Corps. However, for good reasons which completely transcend logic, the United States wants a Marine Corps. Those reasons are strong; they are honest, they are deep rooted and they are above question or criticism. So long as they exist—so long as the people are convinced that we can really do the three things I mentioned—we are going to have a Marine Corps. . . . And, likewise, should the people ever lose that conviction—as a result of our failure to meet their high—almost spiritual standards—the Marine Corps will then quickly disappear.[6]

In 1935, Gunnery Sergeant Walter Holzworth was asked how the Marine Corps came by its reputation as one of the world's greatest fighting formations. He replied, "Well, they started right out telling everybody how great they were. Pretty soon they got to believing it themselves. And they have been busy ever since proving they were right."[7]

Navy

"The profound influence of sea commerce upon the wealth and strength of countries was clearly seen long before the true principles which governed its growth and prosperity were decided," wrote Alfred Thayer Mahan in his classic, *The Influence of Sea Power upon History, 1660–1783*.[8] As Margaret Tuttle Sprout put it, "Mahan's studies convinced him that sea power, conceived on a broader scale, would constitute for the United States . . . an instrument of policy serving to enhance the nation's power and prestige."[9]

Like many other navies, the U.S. Navy has always seen itself intimately tied to national power—protecting it, enhancing it, advancing it. From the seed of this idea has grown the rich heritage that has shaped the way the Navy has done business for centuries on any of "the seven seas." As a seagoing service, the Navy is built on surface ships, submarines, and aircraft, supported by a seaborne logistics force, protecting U.S. interests at sea and on the land immediately adjacent to the sea. Moreover, the culture of the Navy is built on this idea, shaped by—and shaping—this rich heritage.

Those Who Go Down to the Sea in Ships. The Navy—and its Sailors—go to sea. For Sailors, tours at sea and tours ashore are two different things entirely. Sailors often pride themselves, indeed brag about, how many months or years of their careers they have spent at sea. The oceans are vast, so tours at sea are long, usually measured in months rather than weeks. The Navy culture is a *deployment* culture—deployments form the rhythm of Navy life for the Sailors and for their families. If "home is where the heart is," then many, perhaps most, Sailors have two homes, one with family and friends ashore, and the other with shipmates on deployment. The Navy's worldwide presence and availability are its hallmarks, and usually make the Service the first on the scene when trouble erupts affecting U.S. interests in any corner of the globe. To this day, the Navy says, and on some level believes, that when a crisis springs up, the first question the President of the United States asks is, "Where are the carriers?"

Independence. The Navy has always been the most independent of the Services. In its formative years, when a ship went to sea, the Navy cut nearly all of its ties to its place of origin. The often harsh nature of the operating environment at sea forces the Navy to a culture of self-reliance. In the days before modern communications, when the captain of a ship surveyed the horizons from the bridge, he was the master of all he surveyed. There was no one else, including senior officers, there.

Autonomy of Command at Sea. With the captain being the sole word of authority onboard, every decision rested squarely on his shoulders. Even after technology created the ability to "talk to the boss" around the clock, anywhere in the world, the habit of autonomous operations continued to reside in the naval forces. *Command by negation*, a concept unique to naval command and control, allows subordinate commanders the freedom to operate as they see best, keeping authorities informed of decisions made, until the senior overrides a decision. The Navy is the only Service that uses the acronym *UNODIR*—UNless Otherwise DIRected—by which a commanding officer informs the boss of a proposed course of action, and only if the boss overrides it will it not be taken. The subordinate is *informing* the boss, not asking permission.

Community Subcultures. One other important element of Navy culture does not have ancient roots, but is rather a function of the evolution of the Service and, to a great extent, the evolution of technology and hardware. More so than members of the other Services, Sailors identify with a specific warfare specialty or community. The Army has its infantry, artillery, and armor troops, for example, but the powerful identities of the warfare communities in the Navy exceed anything their other comrades in arms know. While some of this power comes from parochialism, there is a more substantial reason for it. No matter their branch, all Soldiers operate on, or near to, the ground. *Land* warfare is their specialty; they work *on the ground.* In contrast, some Sailors operate on the surface of the water, some underneath it, others fly high above it, and still others use the water as the springboard for special operations on land. They think differently because they have to—the varying mediums in which they operate demand it.

Surface Sailors see themselves as the backbone of the naval service, involved in all facets of our nation's defense from power projection ashore to maritime interdiction operations and law enforcement. Submariners take pride in being known as the "Silent Service," referring not only to the stealthiness of their platform, but also to their culture of not discussing their specific operations with others. Since 1910 when the first naval officer was ordered to flight training, naval aviators have assumed an increasingly important role in the Navy, and with it, a style in many ways more like those of their fellow aviators in other Services than like those of their fellow Sailors in other communities. The SEALs (Sea, Air, Land) embody both a flexibility beyond that of their fellow Sailors and a bond between officers and enlisted that is unique within the Navy. This latter is both the reason for and the product of the single Basic Underwater Demolition/SEAL (BUD/S) course that all SEALs— officers and enlisted members—must complete.

Navy–Marine Corps Team. One other element of the Navy culture has to do with the close linkage between it and the Marine Corps. With both branches united under the Department of the Navy, sharing one academy as a commissioning source, and bearing a history of partnership dating back to the 18th century, the Navy–Marine Corps team is able not only to influence events at sea but also to project power ashore, defending and advancing U.S. interests around the world.

Air Force

"Man's flight through life is sustained by the power of his knowledge." These words, written by Austin "Dusty" Miller and inscribed on the Eagle and Fledglings statue at the U.S. Air Force Academy, capture Air Force Service culture. At the heart of this culture is an idea that aviation transformed both civil society and warfare. Aircraft revolutionized war by adding a third dimension to land and sea operations, along with unmatched speed, range, mobility, and flexibility in both combat and support activities. In a like manner, evolving space technology transforms warfare on the Earth's surface. Space capabilities provide revolutionary strides in global presence, intelligence, surveillance, and reconnaissance, communications, geolocation, navigation, weather, and precision weaponry. The airplane and spacecraft also changed society dramatically by opening new horizons of knowledge and shattering previous barriers of time and distance. They made the world smaller. The realities of technology's impact altered profoundly how we travel, how we view the world, and how we fight.

Current Air Force culture emphasizes the term *Airman*. In the past, this word referred to pilots and navigators, but now it refers to anyone who understands and appreciates the full range of air and space capabilities and can employ or support some aspect of airpower and space power.

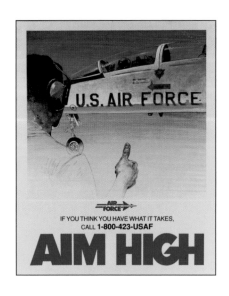

er. The Air Force understands that not all aviators wear a blue uniform; some wear green or khaki or fight from ships. Moreover, not all Airmen are aviators. Nonflying air and space operators, combat support and rescue forces, security forces, and intelligence and logistics troops, and numerous others in "support" functions vitally contribute to air and space superiority. They are all Airmen, and together they form the air and space team.

The concept of independence formed the bedrock of Air Force identity in its early days. Pioneer Airmen believed that the air arm must achieve Service independence in order to operate most effectively and provide the single-minded focus to maximize airpower's potential. At the core of that belief was their understanding, gained through theory and experience, of the strengths and weaknesses of airpower and space power. Early airpower theory stressed *strategic airpower*, that is, the ability to destroy an enemy's warmaking capability by attacking vital centers of industrial or communications infrastructure. Important too was the airplane's capability to provide support to ground troops and air superiority. Indeed, at its inception in 1947 as a distinct and separate Service, the Air Force began with three primary commands: Strategic Air Command, Tactical Air Command, and Air Defense Command.

Although strategic attack, tactical support, and air defense remain important operational functions of airpower and space power, contemporary air and space doctrine emphasizes support to joint and combined operations. It describes the contribution of airpower and space power to the joint warfighting team through "the tenets of air and space power." Air Force Doctrine Document 1, *Air Force Basic Doctrine, Organization, and Command*, describes the tenets of airpower as the "fundamental guiding truths" that reflect not only the unique historical and doctrinal evolution of airpower, but also the specific current understanding of the nature of airpower. These tenets, which are interconnected, overlapping, and often interlocking, emphasize that airpower must:

- be centrally controlled and decentrally executed
- be flexible and versatile
- produce synergistic effects
- offer a unique form of persistence
- be prioritized
- be balanced.

These tenets reflect the specific lessons of air and space operations over history and require informed judgment in application. On the other hand, historically, there were inherent limitations of airpower.

They too were recognized early in the airplane's development:

- technology and capital dependent: not every country has the industrial, scientific, or financial resources to build modern aircraft
- transitory: aircraft cannot live in their medium as surface forces can; they must land to refuel and re-arm
- weather and night: the natural phenomena of rain, wind, clouds, and darkness present formidable barriers to flight
- inability to hold ground: for surface advocates, this is the most damning limitation; only troops can occupy and therefore control events on the ground.

Over the past century of flight, technology enhanced airpower's strengths and diminished its traditional weaknesses. While space assets do not share the same limitations, scientific, technological, and budgetary obstacles pose challenges. Today's Air Force emphasizes mastery of the capabilities and potential of airpower and space power, while understanding fully their limitations. Along the same lines, in order to appreciate Air Force Service culture, the NCO/PO should comprehend the following ideas that mark the Air Force vision.

Unity of Command and Centralized Control/Decentralized Execution. Airmen still believe that the Air Force is the Service most oriented to think in strategic, operational, and tactical dimensions; to think globally; and to appreciate and emphasize time. Hence, Airmen should work for Airmen, and the senior Airman should work for the geographic combatant commander (theater commander) to maximize the capabilities of the joint Service team.

Future-oriented and Technology-focused. Advances in technology dominate both the official and unofficial culture of the Air Force. In one sense, Air Force personnel tend to identify with their plane, space system, or Service specialty. Since it often takes years to master the technology and procedures involved, this cultural trait is natural, but today's Air Force emphasizes a common mission and doctrine to minimize division. Additionally, since rapid technological advances dominate air war, Airmen believe in the words of one of the pioneers of airpower theory, Italian Air Marshal Giulio Douhet: "Victory smiles upon those who anticipate the changes in the character of war, not upon those who wait to adapt themselves after the changes occur."[10]

Space: Unlimited Horizons. With scientific advances opening exciting vistas of space, Douhet's remark captures Air Force thinking for the 21st century. Today's Airman appreciates the value of space as "the ultimate high-ground" and views American space supremacy as an imperative. Today's Air Force is committed to developing tomorrow's space capability in three vital areas: unsurpassed military and civilian space cadre, a strong and consistently funded space industrial base, and commitment to leading-edge space research and exploration. Thus, the Air Force considers itself a genuine air and space force.

Adaptability and Change. From the dawn of flight, Airmen understood the vital role of nonmilitary aviation. The founders of the Air Force consciously developed ties to civilian aerospace industry and the airlines as well as to popular culture in an attempt to develop "air mindedness" and public acceptance. Like civilian industry, the Air Force is based on adaptability and change: new ideas are encouraged, and new management trends are often adopted.

Expeditionary and Forward-deployed. For most of its first 50 years, the Air Force conducted global operations from fixed bases within the continental United States or overseas. With the end of the Cold War and a rise in overseas contingency operations, Air Force culture and operations shifted to an expeditionary, forward-deployed reality. Concentrating on rapid, effective deployment, bare-base operations, and crisis-response actions, the Air and Space Expeditionary Force represents not only a new organization and training focus, but also a new attitude.

With a shorter Service history, fewer cherished traditions, and more emphasis on change, the Air Force often struggles with identity. Airmen master their individual specialties and become highly skilled, but they sometimes become overly specialized, and thus lose perspective on broader Service concerns. Nevertheless, the Air Force prides itself on mission focus and accomplishment. Air Force culture looks to the future and attempts to lead technological trends.

ACTION TODAY

READY ALL WAYS

U.S. COAST GUARD

Coast Guard

In 1790, the First Congress of the United States established a small maritime law enforcement agency to assist in collecting the new nation's customs duties. For the next eight years this Revenue Marine (later called the Revenue Cutter Service) was the nation's only naval force and so was soon assigned military duties. Over time, the Revenue Cutter Service . . . acquired new responsibilities. . . . The result is today's U. S. Coast Guard—a unique force that carries out an array of civil and military responsibilities touching on almost every facet of the maritime environment. . . .

[T]he Coast Guard's legal core is as a military service, invested with unique law enforcement authorities and leavened with a well-earned reputation for humanitarian service. These singular attributes enable us to satisfy a broad, multi-mission mandate from our nation. Our core values of Honor, Respect, and Devotion to Duty are key to fulfilling that mandate.[11]

The Coast Guard's foundation doctrine articulates the essence of the Nation's smallest branch of the Armed Forces. Two hundred plus years as the only armed Service assigned a vast array of civil responsibilities and missions have caused the Coast Guard's culture to be distinctly different from its four larger military cousins. The Nation has long recognized that the Coast Guard requires military discipline and training to perform its national defense duties and its often dangerous maritime security and safety missions successfully. When Alexander Hamilton originally suggested forming the Revenue Marine, he insisted on organizing it along military lines and convinced President George Washington to commission Revenue Marine officers. Thus began the formation of the military culture and history of this small, unique naval Service.

To understand the Coast Guard's unique service culture, one must recognize that it is the compilation of several interrelated histories and cultures. Formed in 1790 as what would later be called the U.S. Revenue Cutter Service, it combined with the U.S. Life-Saving Service in 1915 to form the U.S. Coast Guard. The Coast Guard would later absorb the U.S. Lighthouse Service and Bureau of Maritime Inspection and Navigation. The distinctive service that exists today includes attributes and core values from each organization, expanding and strengthening the Coast Guard's maritime culture. Here are a few highlights of the things that form Coast Guard culture today.

A Naval Service. The Coast Guard is a naval service. It honors the same naval ceremonies, customs, and traditions as its larger sea Service cousins. From the titles it attaches to its ranks and rates to the nautical nomenclature used in everyday speech, the Coast Guard shares a common maritime history with Sailors everywhere. Coastguardsmen have a deep affection for the sea and its lore. Coast Guard cutters are U.S. warships. The Cuttermen who sail in these ships continue a long and distinguished seagoing heritage. Having fought side by side at home and abroad in our nation's conflicts, the Coast Guard is inspired by the history and tradition of the U.S. Navy as well as its own. Every Coastguardsman must remain *Semper Paratus*—Always Ready—to answer the call.

All Things Maritime. The Coast Guard's many roles and missions require it to possess a rare blend of humanitarian, law enforcement, regulatory, diplomatic, and military capabilities. The Coast Guard's many broad regulatory mandates require it to monitor and understand all manner of activity on or near the water. In short, the Coast Guard protects those on the sea, protects Americans against threats delivered by the sea, and protects the sea itself. This omnipresence provides a "cop on the beat" familiarity with the waterfront and a deep understanding of the many occupations and enterprises that make their living on or around the sea. A long, distinguished history of enforcing international maritime treaties and successful joint naval operations extends this comprehensive knowledge and understanding of all things maritime far beyond the borders of the United States.

Face-to-face Interaction with the Citizens It Serves. The Coast Guard's many civil, peacetime missions require it to have far greater day-to-day interaction with the American public than the other branches of the Armed Forces. From rescuing a recreational boater in distress to conducting an inspection on a large merchant ship, many citizens have reason to have routine contact with Coast Guard personnel. This frequent interaction presents extraordinary challenges for the organization and individual Coastguardsman. Coast Guard personnel must exercise their powers prudently and with restraint. In his 1791 Letter of Instruction to Revenue Cutter officers, Alexander Hamilton charged them to "overcome difficulties . . . by a cool and temperate perseverance in [your] duty."[12] That standard remains integral to Coast Guard culture today.

Small Units in Small Places. The Coast Guard has very few large bases. It is an organization dominated by small boat stations, small cutters (ships), and small air stations—often in equally small coastal communities far from other military facilities. These small units are integral parts of the community. Often operating far from higher command authority, junior Coast Guard leaders, including POs, enjoy a clear mandate for on-scene initiative, but also bear immense responsibility for the well-being and conduct of their crews.

"You Have to Go Out but You Don't Have to Come Back." Coastguardsmen are taught to avoid or mitigate unnecessary risk, but this historic, deep-rooted saying from the U.S. Life-Saving Service captures the Coast Guard's heritage of selfless service to the Nation. Whether it is combat, law enforcement, or search-and-rescue operations, the Coast Guard does dangerous work in hostile environments. Selfless acts by courageous men and women using their tools and their wits under dangerous conditions to get the job done are the foundation of Coast Guard culture. A lifeboat crashing through the surf or a helicopter in a low hover over a vessel in distress are the enduring images of the Coast Guard at work.

Maritime Cop on the Beat. Maritime law enforcement and border control are the oldest of the Coast Guard's many responsibilities and the historic core of its existence. Stopping and boarding ships at sea

Sergeant Alvin C. York, 328th Infantry, who with the aid of 7 men captured 132 German prisoners, shows the hill on which the raid took place on October 8, 1918, in the Argonne Forest, near Cornay, France, after World War I (F.C. Phillips)

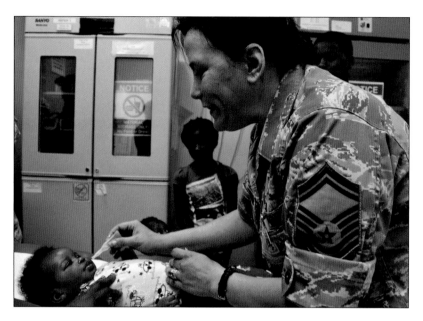

Air Force Senior Master Sergeant Virginia Westover with the 179ᵗʰ Medical Group works at the immunizations and allergy office of the 48ᵗʰ Medical Group Medical Support Squadron at RAF Lakenheath, England, June 19, 2013 (Joe Harwood)

Marine Heavy Helicopter Squadron 464 assists Marines of 2nd Reconnaissance Battalion conduct special purpose insertion and extraction training aboard Marine Corps Base Camp Lejeune, North Carolina, March 13, 2013 (Ryan Joyner)

The Sullivan brothers were five siblings all killed in action during or shortly after the sinking of the light cruiser USS Juneau *(CL-52), the vessel on which they all served, around November 13, 1942, in World War II*

Coast Guard Petty Officer 2nd Class Shawn Beaty looks for survivors in the wake of Hurricane Katrina in New Orleans, Louisiana, August 30, 2005 (NyxoLyno Cangemi)

Staff Sergeant Antonio J. Curry, a drill instructor aboard Marine Corps Recruit Depot San Diego, barks out instructions to align his platoon of fresh recruits, August 30, 2012 (Kuande Hall)

A member of the 3rd U.S. Infantry, The Old Guard, inspects a relieving guard's rifle before his watch at the Tomb of the Unknown Soldier, Arlington National Cemetery, January 9, 2008 (Michael Russell)

Sergeant 1st Class Lawrence Jarrett (left), of Spencer, Oklahoma, Sergeant 1st Class Jared Hallmark (center), of Choctaw, Oklahoma, and Master Sergeant Ken Perry (right), of Shawnee, Oklahoma, review a map of the area they are about to search for a missing 3-year-old boy. All three are members of the 63rd Civil Support Team, Oklahoma National Guard. The missing boy was pulled from his house by a tornado on May 24, 2013 (Geoff Legler)

A grief-stricken American infantryman whose buddy has been killed in action is comforted by another Soldier. In the background, a corpsman methodically fills out casualty tags, Haktong-ni area, Korea, August 28, 1950 (Al Chang)

Lance Corporal Ashley Ramirez and Corporal Jessica L. Echeard of the Regimental Combat Team–2 Lioness Program check the passports of Iraqi women coming into the country at the Syrian Border in Waleed, Iraq, June 7, 2007. The Lionesses is an all-female unit organized to engage with Iraqi women at entry control points (Charles S. Howard)

Navy chief petty officers celebrate 120 years of the chief petty officer rank, April 1, 2013, at the U.S. Navy Memorial in Washington, DC (Todd Frantom)

Technical Sergeant Eddie Martin provides maintenance status to pilots prior to their acceptance of the aircraft for flight operations (Marleah Miller)

Lieutenant Colonel John Hopkins, commanding officer of the First Battalion, Fifth Marine Regiment, leads in singing the "The Star-Spangled Banner" during memorial services held in the field during the Korean campaign, June 21, 1951 (Corporal Valle)

Joseph Ambrose, an 86-year-old World War I veteran, attends the dedication day parade for the Vietnam Veterans Memorial in Washington, DC, November 13, 1982. He is holding the flag that covered the casket of his son, who was killed in the Korean War (Mickey Sanborn)

Chief Master Sergeant Curtis Brownhill (left), command senior enlisted advisor of U.S. Central Command, stands atop a patrol base in Tarmiya, Iraq, with Command Sergeant Ronald Riling, 4th Infantry Division, August 21, 2006. Brownhill visited troops throughout the Baghdad area bringing words of encouragement and an open ear to Soldiers' concerns (Karl Johnson)

Coast Guard Petty Officer 3rd Class Brice Fronek, with Coast Guard Cutter Bernard C. Webber, *guards contraband at Coast Guard Base Miami Beach, April 26, 2013. The contraband was seized during an interdiction in the Caribbean Sea, April 18, 2013 (Sabrina Laberdesque)*

provided the foundation upon which the Coast Guard's broader and more complex present-day mission set is built. The burden of being the Nation's primary maritime law enforcement service is an essential and inescapable component of Coast Guard culture.

The Coast Guard's relatively small size, assignment within the Department of Homeland Security, and civil responsibilities and missions make its culture and authorities unique among the U.S. Armed Forces. As stated in Coast Guard Publication 1, *U.S. Coast Guard: America's Maritime Guardian*, "What makes the Coast Guard unique is that in executing our diverse missions, we harmonize seemingly contradictory mandates. We are charged at once to be police officers, sailors, warriors, humanitarians, regulators, stewards of the environment, diplomats, and guardians of the coast."[13]

Guard and Reserve

To keep the United States secure and to protect its vital interests across the globe, the Armed Forces rely on a Total Force construct composed of both Active-duty and Reserve components. The Reserve components consist of the Army Reserve, Navy Reserve, Marine Corps Reserve, Air Force Reserve, Coast Guard Reserve, Army National Guard of the United States, and Air National Guard of the United States. The purpose of the Reserve components, as prescribed by law, is to "provide trained units and qualified persons available for active duty in the armed forces, in time of war or national emergency . . . whenever more units and persons are needed than are in the regular components."[15]

The Reserve components are commensurately organized, trained, and equipped as their Active-duty counterparts, and over recent decades have steadily transformed from a strategic reserve to a fully operational force capable of seamlessly integrating with Active-duty forces for roles across the spectrum of conflict and engagement. They play a vital role in the global security environment through both integrated missions with Active-duty forces, as well as specialized missions that the Reserve component is uniquely suited for and fully prepared to perform. They not only integrate with Active forces operationally, but they uniquely represent the Armed Forces' closest link to the American public through their roles within their communities.

Members of the various Army National Guard, Air National Guard, and Service Reserve forces share the culture and heritage of their Services, but in at least three ways their cultures are somewhat different from that of their Active component brothers and sisters.

First, most Guardsmen and Reservists spend most of their lives as part of the broader civilian population, and thus serve as *military ambassadors to the American people.* Unless activated for a specific purpose, they spend 1 weekend a month and 2 weeks a year as full-time Soldiers, Marines, Sailors, Airmen, and Coastguardsmen. People who join the Guard or Reserves maintain their full-time civilian employment while serving on weekends, completing training, and ultimately deploying. They make this choice knowing the hardships of balancing family commitments, civilian employment, and military obligations.

National Guard armories and Reserve bases are located in more than 3,000 communities across the United States. Guard and Reserve members are located in nearly every congressional district. They have links to their local civic and elected leadership, with relationships developed in schools, churches, clubs, sports, and civic organizations. They are responsible for telling the military's story to the vast majority of the American people who have never served. They also help ensure that a more diverse military population is better aware of, and connected to, the citizens it serves.

Second, National Guardsmen have a distinctive role as *ambassadors abroad* through the State Partnership Program (SPP). With partnerships with 65 foreign countries, located in all six geographic combatant commands, the National Guard's SPP builds enduring relationships that meet U.S. global security objectives. This innovative, low-cost, and high-impact program delivers a significant return on investment by motivating partner countries to share in the burden of global security. For over 20 years, National Guard members and their partner country counterparts have focused on small footprint activities, including exercises, rotational presence, and advisory services to achieve security objectives. Servicemembers often forge relationships with partner countries that last throughout their careers. Some partner countries observed the U.S. military's model of empowering NCOs/POs to take on a greater share of leadership responsibilities and decided to apply it in their own armed forces.

Third, Army and Air National Guardsmen can serve in several different legal statuses: state Active duty (SAD), Title 32, and Title 10 of the U.S. Code. They can have two different commanders in chief: their state governor and the President of the United States.

SAD allows militia members to perform their military duties within their respective states without violating Federal laws, such as the *Posse Comitatus Act*, which normally prohibits law enforcement by military personnel. This legal status provides the governor with an option to use militia members for law enforcement purposes within the state. The governor of each state retains command and control over the National Guard forces called to state Active duty. Thus, in contrast with their Active-duty counterparts, Guardsmen are more solidly anchored in their respective states.

Title 32 of the U.S. Code is another attractive flexible legal option particular to the National Guard. Under this legal provision, militia members serve on Active duty for a specific Federal purpose. Following the 9/11 attacks, for example, National Guard members provided security details at airports within their states in Title 32 status after being called upon by the President. Out of all legal statuses, Title 32 offers states the most flexibility, insofar as it allows the governor to retain control over the state's own militia while ensuring that the Federal Government subsidizes the costs of activating the force.

Finally, the President can call the National Guard to Active duty under Title 10. Federalizing the National Guard places control of the forces under the President as Commander in Chief, just like any other

Federal force. A federalized National Guard member is no different from an Active-duty member with same rights and protections.

Conclusion

These five powerful Services, as well as the Guard and Reserves, are diverse but complementary, and together they constitute the Armed Forces of the United States. The challenge for NCOs/POs is to be simultaneously masters of their own Services *and* knowledgeable partners of the others. Taking appropriate pride in one's own Service is in order, but that should never stray into arrogance regarding the other Services. *Different* does not mean *inferior*; it means different. The talented, professional NCO/PO—at any pay grade—must be ready, willing, and able to leverage the best of each of the Services as the mission requires.

Joint warfighting is the employment of the Armed Forces in a common effort to achieve a desired end. Joint warfighting is not new. George Washington's victory at Yorktown depended on cooperation with naval forces, that is, the French fleet. Ulysses S. Grant's victories on the western rivers were built largely on Navy cooperation with Army forces onshore. The great amphibious landings of World War II could not have taken place without imaginative and detailed integration of the efforts and complementary capabilities of all the Nation's military forces.

What has changed in the 21ˢᵗ century is the overlapping nature of individual Service capabilities within a single area of operations. Essentially, the range of weapons and communication systems, combined with the ability to create and operate sophisticated information networks, promises to reduce the theater of war to a single battlespace on which effects created by forces of all Services can be employed selectively and simultaneously throughout the area, much as Napoleon Bonaparte directed subordinate units around early 19ᵗʰ-century battlefields.

As Napoleon's cavalry, artillery, and infantry retained unique characteristics because of differences in capabilities, operating requirements, and skills, so today's military Services necessarily retain their unique identities, founded on their histories and on the continuing differences in the functional requirements of operating in their respective mediums. Conflicting pressures—full operational integration of effects for greatest collective impact and organizational separation to maximize individual means—have required the development of new organizational concepts to guide the Services in achieving the greatest possible operational integration, while maintaining their more or less traditional organizational diversity.

Central to 21st-century warfare is the concept of *joint interdependence*, which is broadly the notion that Service capabilities provided to joint operational commanders are combined to achieve their full complementary effects, at the lowest possible level, to obtain the greatest possible collective effects. Achieving joint interdependence requires that officers and NCOs/POs alike understand the differing strengths and limitations of each Service's capabilities and know-how to integrate them in order to speed mission accomplishment. Service rivalries have no place on the battlefield, where success, not credit, is the professional currency.

Because seamless cooperation at all levels is increasingly important, reciprocal respect of members of other Services as fellow warriors and members of the Profession of Arms is vital. Operational integration begins with mutual understanding and respect, as well as shared adherence to the professional military ethic born out of the Oath of Enlistment, which this book invokes as common ground for all noncommissioned officers and petty officers. Joint synergy, the ability to make the whole greater than the sum of the parts, begins with understanding the several Service cultures. *E pluribus unum.*

Notes

[1] "Original design of the Great Seal of the United States (1782)," available at <www.ourdocuments.gov/doc.php?flash=true&doc=5>.

[2] R.L. Brownlee and Peter J. Schoomaker, *United States Army 2004 Posture Statement*, Presented to the Committees and Subcommittees of the United States Senate and the House of Representatives, 108th Cong., 2nd sess. (Washington, DC: Office of the Chief of Staff, U.S. Army, Special Actions Branch, February 5, 2004), 1, available at <www.army.mil/aps/04/index.html>.

[3] T.R. Fehrenback, *This Kind of War: A Study in Unpreparedness* (New York: Macmillan, 1963), quoted in Field Manual 3-0, *Operations* (Washington, DC: Headquarters Department of the Army, June 14, 2001), 1–2.

[4] War Department, Adjutant General's Office, Washington, April 24, 1863, General Orders No. 100, "Instructions for the Government of Armies of the United States in the Field," prepared by Francis Lieber, LLD, and revised by a board of officers, of

which Major General E.A. Hitchcock is president . . . in War Department, *The War of the Rebellion: A Compilation of the Official Records of the Union and Confederate Armies*, Series III, Volume III (Washington, DC: Government Printing Office, 1899), 150.

[5] Marine Corps Warfighting Publication 6-11, *Leading Marines* (Washington, DC: Headquarters United States Marine Corps, 1995), 3

[6] Victor H. Krulak, *First to Fight: An Inside View of the United States Marine Corps* (New York: Pocket Books, 1984), xix–xxi.

[7] Ibid., 1

[8] Alfred Thayer Mahan, *The Influence of Sea Power upon History, 1660–1783* (New York: Dover Publications, 1987), 1.

[9] Margaret Tuttle Sprout, "Mahan: Evangelist of Seapower," in *The Art and Practice of Military Strategy*, ed. George Edward Thibault, 114 (Washington, DC: National Defense University, 1984).

[10] Giulio Douhet, *The Command of the Air*, trans. Dino Ferrari (New York: Coward-McCann, 1942; reprint, Washington, DC: Office of Air Force History, 1983), 30.

[11] Coast Guard Publication 1, *U.S. Coast Guard: America's Maritime Guardian* (Washington, DC: U.S. Coast Guard, 2009), 1, 73–74.

[12] Ibid., 88.

[13] Ibid., 1.

[14] Bruce Stubbs, "We Are Lifesavers, Guardians, and Warriors," U.S. Naval Institute *Proceedings* (April 2002).

[15] United States Code, 2006 Edition, Section 10102, Title 10—ARMED FORCES, available at <www.gpo.gov/fdsys/granule/USCODE-2011-title10/USCODE-2011-title10-subtitleE-partI-chap1003-sec10102/content-detail.html>.

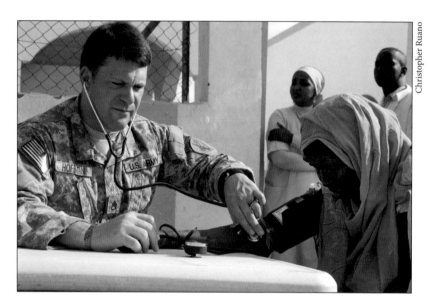

Staff Sergeant Matthew Hoffman, 448th Civil Affairs Battalion noncommissioned officer in charge of operations, performs a blood pressure check on a patient during a Medical Civic Action Program clinic in Chebelley, Djibouti, October 6, 2012

CHAPTER SEVEN

International Roles

Our ability to sustain . . . alliances, and to build coalitions of support toward common objectives, depends in part on the capabilities of America's Armed Forces. Similarly, the relationships our Armed Forces have developed with foreign militaries are a critical component of our global engagement and support our collective security.

We will continue to ensure that we can prevail against a wide range of potential adversaries—to include hostile states and nonstate actors—while broadly shaping the strategic environment using all tools to advance our common security.

—National Security Strategy[1]

The U.S. Armed Forces play a vital role in the global security environment. Drawing on the professional traits, qualities, and competencies developed within their respective Service branches and enriched through experience, exposure, and engagement, the noncommissioned officer/petty officer corps greatly contributes to meeting America's national security objectives in diverse environments. Furthermore, as leaders in the Profession of Arms, their roles, responsibilities, authorities, and innovative methods of operating can provide a model for other countries to emulate.

The 21st-century global security environment differs greatly from the environment of yesteryear. It is marked by remarkable complexity, ambiguity, evolution, and transformation. Among the factors shaping this environment are shifting demographics, interdependent economies, competition for natural resources, global natural disasters, and, in several parts of the globe, the aspirations of newly emerging contenders for regional and global influence. Advances in technology and communications both improve and threaten this evolving and transforming security environment. Emerging security threats and challenges include often unpredictable failed states, international criminal and terrorist networks, and other nonstate actors. In this fluctuating context, the global community must think collectively about new ways and means to deter, dissuade, or defeat these threats through unity of effort and innovative security arrangements.

Serving in alliances, coalitions, and partnerships is woven into the fabric of the U.S. Armed Forces. From the inception of the Nation, Americans have relied on, and provided aid or assistance to, other countries. Beginning in the second half of the 20th century, the United States has worked within international organizations such as the United Nations and has entered into a wide variety of security arrangements, from multinational alliances, often bound by formal treaties for enduring mutual defense, to less formally bound multinational coalitions, with specific purposes and generally limited durations. Maintaining international alliances or coalitions requires a collective vision of mission, flexibility, and adaptability, and a continuing effort by all leaders to keep the alliance or coalition strong and confident. Often, keeping the coalition focused and unified is as important as the operation itself. General John P. Abizaid, USA, then-commander of U.S. Central Command, captured this idea well in 2005 when he told his senior staff and the senior national representatives of the coalition supporting the war on terror: "Nothing is as important as the Coalition in this battle."[2]

Irrespective of the strategic framework, or the size and scope of any security arrangement the United States may enter into, the Nation will leverage the Armed Forces to engage with its partners. Whether in combat or in a humanitarian role, the United States, its allies, and partners have always depended on the specialized skills, expertise, and leadership capabilities of its professional enlisted force. Forged in crisis and reinforced during decades of peace, the history of NCOs/POs in international affairs is deeply rooted in a resilient personal determination, persistent resolve, and a strong set of professional standards and ethics. This international legacy transcends generations and instills in today's NCOs/POs a high sense of global purpose and a positive bias toward solidarity with the militaries of other nations working with the United States.

In this new century, not only are NCOs/POs depended on to perform their traditional roles with credibility and efficiency, but they are also leveraged and empowered to perform strategic roles in this evolving global security environment. NCOs/POs are uniquely adept at advising, training, and mentoring others at various levels of military organization and structure. Moreover, NCOs/POs are critical in helping other nations' militaries to achieve new or increased levels of capability, especially at the small unit and individual levels, and to meet emerging or evolving challenges where interpersonal skills, the warrior ethos, and diplomatic approaches are necessities.

NCOs/POs, regardless of specialty or background, may find themselves involved directly in a wide range of international engagements—from major combat to various forms of international security force assistance operations to humanitarian relief. They may be involved in multilateral or bilateral exercises, military assistance activities, and even large-scale engagements. NCOs/POs may be assigned to an alliance delegation, a coalition battle staff, a multinational force headquarters, an Embassy, or a personnel exchange program. Almost assuredly, they will be connected with whole-of-government endeavors, working hand in hand with other U.S. Government agencies, nongovernmental organizations, and ministries of defense in pursuit of common goals. In each case, NCOs/POs can and do facilitate professional relationships that can yield an enduring positive strategic effect.

The NCO/PO leadership cadre is the closest to the force and will have the greatest immediate impact on accomplishing organizational milestones. NCOs/POs keep things in proper perspective, and they help maintain a positive and productive organizational climate through an acute understanding of the mission and a keen sense of inclusiveness, not only for U.S. forces, but also for those of other nations. They foster mutual trust and confidence in a multi-Service and multinational force, recognizing that troops of any Service or nation will follow an engaged leader who genuinely cares about them and appreciates their contribution to the organization.

In addition to their involvement with multinational alliances and coalitions, NCOs/POs directly contribute to fostering partnerships with other nations on behalf of the United States. As former Secretary of Defense Robert Gates wrote, "This strategic reality demands that the U.S. government get better at what is called 'building partner capacity': helping other countries defend themselves or, if necessary, fight alongside U.S. forces by providing them with equipment, training, or other forms of security assistance."[3]

An Ambassador and a Professional

The American people have exceptionally high expectations for their military, especially when serving overseas as the face of the United States and the ambassadors of its citizens. They expect that their military will ably represent the society it serves and the ideals on which the Nation was founded. Americans further expect their military to maintain high moral standards, embody the Code of Conduct, and personify the standards, traits, qualities, and competencies of a member of the Profession of Arms. As trusted leaders of the all-volunteer force, NCOs/POs lead their subordinates to exceed these expectations, and they do so through personal example, inspiration, and enforcement. General Martin E. Dempsey, Chairman of the Joint Chiefs of Staff, defined the expectations of Americans for their military members this way: "We must provide an example to the world that cannot be diminished by hardships and challenges. This example is based upon the words and intent of the U.S. Constitution that each of us takes a personal oath to support and defend. Our oath demands each of us display moral courage and always do what is right, regardless of the cost."[4]

NCOs/POs can justifiably lay claim to a long and impressive history of contributing to success in managing and resolving international crises, and partnering with other militaries during peacetime and conflict. U.S. military personnel are judged by their deeds, including when dealing with other nations. NCOs/POs serving in alliances, coalitions, and security partnerships must remain true to who they are, while bringing out the best in others. NCOs/POs bring with them the values and strategic objectives of the United States, as well as the traits, qualities, and competencies of the Profession of Arms. Whether stationed abroad (often with their families), enjoying a port of call, or attached to an international force, the enlisted leader understands that every engagement can have strategic effects and that those who wear the uniform are representing the United States. Their conduct must be above reproach. NCOs/POs take all appropriate measures to ensure that military members are professional at all times and respectful of other cultures, peoples, and societies.

At the same time, NCOs/POs must remember those times when events have not gone well for the U.S. military or the United States. From violation of a status-of-forces agreement to some form of inappropriate conduct by an individual or small group, these incidents result in significant strategic setbacks and international embarrassment. As an institution, the Armed Forces do not relish highlighting such occurrences in which the conduct of a tiny percentage of the force tarnishes the honorable reputation and ethical service of the military as a whole. However, all members of the Profession of Arms must be personally reflective, open to national and international scrutiny, and dedicated to preserving the integrity of the Profession of Arms by policing its ranks.

Proven leadership throughout the NCO/PO corps provides a solid foundation for engaging with foreign counterparts. Over the years, the fine work of NCOs/POs with extensive experience in international military assistance and building partnership capacity has yielded many best practices worthy of study and emulation. A great deal can be gleaned from U.S. Special Forces, who for many decades have been intimately involved with training, advising, and mentoring international militaries. Working at the operational and tactical levels, special operations forces NCOs/POs maintain a high degree of strategic awareness, which makes them especially well equipped to take on engagement activities. In building international partnership capacity, and in contributing to professionalizing other militaries, the most effective NCOs/POs are critical and creative thinkers who keep a wider view of the environment, and who are extremely adaptive when empowered in diverse, highly decentralized situations. They maintain a keen understanding of the "human element." Seeing through the eyes of others is a powerful way to learn and thus gain the trust and garner the respect of those of other cultures and traditions.

Building Partner Capacity

In these situations, a high degree of mutual respect, openness, inclusiveness, and patience is critical. NCOs/POs are mindful that the servicemembers of other nations are equally proud of their own countries. NCOs/POs appreciate different national visions, cultures, traditions, sensitivities, loyalties, and motivations whether they are political, tribal, or religious. They seek what is common among military professionals and get to know the people they are working with. They understand that no two countries are alike and that regions vary in any number of ways. Thus, any developmental or professionalization approaches must be calibrated to be effective for each particular country. To this end, NCOs/POs familiarize themselves with that nation's defense structures, force foundations (volunteer or conscript), rank structures, and levels of responsibilities and authorities of the force. They respect the other nation's institutions and customs and show appropriate courtesies to its officers and other leaders. When focusing efforts on professionalizing mid-level leadership, NCOs/POs understand that many other militaries may not have a professional NCO/PO corps. Therefore, NCOs/POs may find themselves advising and mentoring another country's officer corps to win access, support, and buy-in for developing a corps of professional mid-level leaders.

In working with other nations' militaries, it is paramount to understand and appreciate that NCOs/POs both learn from and teach others. Effective U.S. advisors, trainers, and mentors understand that they must learn from others and that they will gain understanding by listening. There is no immediate benefit or strategic advantage in attempting to replicate the U.S. military model. While the U.S. structure is superb in many ways, and can be a distinctive model, other nations have different circumstances and requirements. NCOs/POs are at their best when they show other militaries what is good, effective, and efficient in the U.S. Armed Forces model and then pursue meaningful discussions and courses of action toward what makes best sense for that nation's military. NCOs/POs help another nation's military leaders understand what is right for *their* country as opposed to attempting to recast another nation's military into a mirror image of the U.S. military. Competence, credibility, capability, and character build *trust*. When military leaders in other nations recognize these professional traits, qualities, and competencies in U.S. advisors, trainers, and mentors, they are more inclined to cooperate, thus setting the conditions to move forward in security partnerships and arrangements that serve the near-term and even longer term interest of all participating nations.

NCOs/POs continue to play vital roles in attaining the national security objectives of the United States. Sergeant Major of the Army Raymond F. Chandler III underscored this point to Army NCOs: "Forging bonds with the Soldiers of other countries can pay big dividends as our Army engages in regional alignments and builds partner capacity. NCOs can have an impact across the entire spectrum of operations." Service to one's nation is what is common to the Profession of Arms. As the U.S. Armed Forces' premier advisors, trainers, and mentors, NCOs/POs will increasingly be called on to serve alongside, and also to provide a professional example for, international forces in multinational alliances and coalitions, to assist in building partnership capacity, and to contribute to innovative approaches to foreign affairs. To meet the known and emerging requirements of the international environment, the U.S. noncommissioned officer and petty officer will need to possess a global vision and an adaptive mind—as well as professional and personal traits, qualities, and competencies—to positively influence and operate with international militaries. They will need to do so while striking a necessary and desirable balance between traditional U.S. military culture and identity and the unique partnership requirements of an international force.

Notes

[1] *National Security Strategy* (Washington, DC: The White House, May 2010), 41, available at <www.whitehouse.gov/sites/default/files/rss_viewer/national_security_strategy.pdf>.

[2] General John P. Abizaid, commander, U.S. Central Command (2003–2007), Guidance and Intent during 2005 strategy focus session with field commanders, commanders, and senior U.S. and coalition staff as recorded by U.S. Central Command senior enlisted advisor.

[3] Robert M. Gates, "Helping Others Defend Themselves: The Future of U.S. Security Assistance," *Foreign Affairs*, May/June 2010, available at <www.foreignaffairs.com/articles/66224/robert-m-gates/helping-others-defend-themselves>.

[4] Martin E. Dempsey, "America's Military—A Profession of Arms," 3, available at <www.jcs.mil/content/files/2012-02/022312120752_Americas_Military_POA.pdf>.

Command Sergeant Major Sherman Fuller, USA (Ret.), teaches a group of students at the Global Village Academy in Colorado Springs, Colorado, where he serves as principal

Afterword
The Service Continues

Whether serving for 4 years or 4 decades, those who have honorably worn the cloth of the Nation as invested members of the Profession of Arms are eternally associated with this battle-proven, dynamic, and highly respected organization known as the United States Armed Forces.

Those who make this commitment are the protectors of their fellow citizens and the defenders of freedom and liberty. For over 200 years, they have come from all walks of life—from big cities, small towns, suburbia, and rural communities—and are all bound together by duty to pursue a common purpose: the safety, security, and freedom of their nation. These men and women view the American flag not only as an emblem of geographical vastness and diversity, but also as the symbol of what the United States of America stands for, what its values and ideals are, and what it considers worth fighting and dying for. They *have stood the watch* in an uncertain world with vigilance, devotion, and courage. Their commitment to their fellow Servicemembers is exemplified by *never leaving a fallen comrade*. Their lives are enriched by discipline, obedience, comradeship, and teamwork and by the sure knowledge that they are a part of something that is above and beyond their individual lives. Not that long ago it was common to hear a veteran say, "I was in the service"—meaning *in service to the Nation*.

A lifelong loyalty often comes with this commitment to serve the Nation—a conscious and free choice to continue to serve even after returning to civilian life. This loyalty stems from one's personal experience performing a demanding duty to which few have obligated themselves—the larger, deeper, and meaningful duty of service and sacrifice for the welfare of others.

For some, service continues as soon as they return to civilian life. For others, the call to continue to serve comes later. In either case, that service may take many forms. Most who have served and have departed the ranks and files of the Armed Forces reintegrate back into American society and choose to serve in new ways. Some choose to continue to serve by taking civilian jobs in government service at the Federal, state, or local level. Some offer themselves as candidates for elective office. Many join veterans' organizations to maintain those precious bonds with others who have worn the cloth of the Nation or civic organizations that help sustain and nurture local communities. Others work with young people as teachers, coaches, or Junior Reserve Officer Training Corps instructors, guiding a younger generation toward lives of service. Some obligate themselves to direct military support organizations as leaders or volunteers. Others visit wounded warriors to provide strength and encouragement or volunteer at Veterans Administration hospitals or homeless shelters. Still others volunteer to serve in details that render military honors at veterans' funerals, provide escort services for fallen comrades, or routinely mow the lawn of a deployed Servicemember's home. No matter the particulars, what these and other forms of continuing service have in common is the idea of "service before self."

Yet veterans who do not choose to continue service in such visible ways still stand out. They are often family members or neighbors who, because of their experience and discipline, are sought out for leadership when an emergency arises. They can also be a source of "Civics 101." They can explain how and why some things are not free—that the few serve the many. They participate in national days of recognition and patriotism and attend their Services' birthday celebrations, singing their Services' songs loudly and proudly. They are the ones who respect Old Glory as the flag parades by. For them, it is more than a bumper sticker on a vehicle or a unit patch on a ball cap that denotes time of service. It is a manifestation of pride in the sacrifice that is required as a member of the Profession of Arms in times of peace and war.

Those who "stood the watch" before today's Servicemembers provide an enduring example of patriotism and service. The Marine Corps motto of *Semper Fidelis* (Latin for "always faithful") can speak to every member of the Profession of Arms. Those who have worn the uniform of the Nation should never tarnish the reputation or the legacy that was paid for with the blood of so many for the future of so many more. "Soldier for Life" means exactly what it says. And there is no more patriotic optic for America to witness than the 85-year-old retired NCO Ranger who is propping himself up in his wheelchair as the national colors march by. He does not do it for a photograph; he does it because he still *feels* Army.

The most quoted portion of President John F. Kennedy's inaugural address exemplifies the service to one's country that continues to inspire the members of the Armed Forces, while in uniform and after they return to civilian life: "Ask not what your country can do for you—ask what you can do for your country."[1] Veterans set an example of a higher calling, and they demonstrate tangibly and proudly that, even though they have departed a Service, *service* has not departed them. This sense of service exemplifies the loyalty and lifelong commitment of those who were willing, if necessary, to give the "last full measure of devotion" in the service of a grateful nation. This is yet another reason why the United States Armed Forces is America's most respected and honored profession.

Note

  [1] John F. Kennedy, Inaugural Address, Washington, DC, January 20, 1961, available at <www.jfklibrary.org/>.

Appendix A: Founding Documents

THE DECLARATION OF INDEPENDENCE

IN CONGRESS, July 4, 1776.

The unanimous Declaration of the thirteen united States of America,

When in the Course of human events, it becomes necessary for one people to dissolve the political bands which have connected them with another, and to assume among the powers of the earth, the separate and equal station to which the Laws of Nature and of Nature's God entitle them, a decent respect to the opinions of mankind requires that they should declare the causes which impel them to the separation.

We hold these truths to be self-evident, that all men are created equal, that they are endowed by their Creator with certain unalienable Rights, that among these are Life, Liberty and the pursuit of Happiness.—That to secure these rights, Governments are instituted among Men, deriving their just powers from the consent of the governed, —That whenever any Form of Government becomes destructive of these ends, it is the Right of the People to alter or to abolish it, and to institute new Government, laying its foundation on such principles and organizing its powers in such form, as to them shall seem most likely to effect their Safety and Happiness. Prudence, indeed, will dictate that Governments long established should not be changed for light and transient causes; and accordingly all experience hath shewn, that mankind are more disposed to suffer, while evils are sufferable, than to right themselves by abolishing the forms to which they are accustomed. But when a long train of abuses and usurpations, pursuing invariably the same Object evinces a design to reduce them under absolute Despotism, it is their right, it is their duty, to throw off such Government, and to provide new Guards for their future security.—Such has been the patient sufferance of these Colonies; and such is now the necessity which constrains them to alter their former Systems of Government. The history of the present King of Great Britain is a history of repeated injuries and usurpations, all having in direct object the establishment of an absolute Tyranny over these States. To prove this, let Facts be submitted to a candid world.

He has refused his Assent to Laws, the most wholesome and necessary for the public good.

He has forbidden his Governors to pass Laws of immediate and pressing importance, unless suspended in their operation till his Assent should be obtained; and when so suspended, he has utterly neglected to attend to them.

He has refused to pass other Laws for the accommodation of large districts of people, unless those people would relinquish the right of Representation in the Legislature, a right inestimable to them and formidable to tyrants only.

He has called together legislative bodies at places unusual, uncomfortable, and distant from the depository of their public Records, for the sole purpose of fatiguing them into compliance with his measures.

He has dissolved Representative Houses repeatedly, for opposing with manly firmness his invasions on the rights of the people.

He has refused for a long time, after such dissolutions, to cause others to be elected; whereby the Legislative powers, incapable of Annihilation, have returned to the People at large for their exercise; the State remaining in the mean time exposed to all the dangers of invasion from without, and convulsions within.

He has endeavoured to prevent the population of these States; for that purpose obstructing the Laws for Naturalization of Foreigners; refusing to pass others to encourage their migrations hither, and raising the conditions of new Appropriations of Lands.

He has obstructed the Administration of Justice, by refusing his Assent to Laws for establishing Judiciary powers.

He has made Judges dependent on his Will alone, for the tenure of their offices, and the amount and payment of their salaries.

He has erected a multitude of New Offices, and sent hither swarms of Officers to harrass our people, and eat out their substance.

He has kept among us, in times of peace, Standing Armies without the Consent of our legislatures.

He has affected to render the Military independent of and superior to the Civil power.

He has combined with others to subject us to a jurisdiction foreign to our constitution, and unacknowledged by our laws; giving his Assent to their Acts of pretended Legislation:

For Quartering large bodies of armed troops among us:

For protecting them, by a mock Trial, from punishment for any Murders which they should commit on the Inhabitants of these States:

For cutting off our Trade with all parts of the world:

For imposing Taxes on us without our Consent:

For depriving us in many cases, of the benefits of Trial by Jury:

For transporting us beyond Seas to be tried for pretended offences

For abolishing the free System of English Laws in a neighbouring Province, establishing therein an Arbitrary government, and enlarging its Boundaries so as to render it at once an example and fit instrument for introducing the same absolute rule into these Colonies:

For taking away our Charters, abolishing our most valuable Laws, and altering fundamentally the Forms of our Governments:

For suspending our own Legislatures, and declaring themselves invested with power to legislate for us in all cases whatsoever.

He has abdicated Government here, by declaring us out of his Protection and waging War against us.

He has plundered our seas, ravaged our Coasts, burnt our towns, and destroyed the lives of our people.

He is at this time transporting large Armies of foreign Mercenaries to compleat the works of death, desolation and tyranny, already begun with circumstances of Cruelty & perfidy scarcely paralleled in the most barbarous ages, and totally unworthy the Head of a civilized nation.

He has constrained our fellow Citizens taken Captive on the high Seas to bear Arms against their Country, to become the executioners of their friends and Brethren, or to fall themselves by their Hands.

He has excited domestic insurrections amongst us, and has endeavoured to bring on the inhabitants of our frontiers, the merciless Indian Savages, whose known rule of warfare, is an undistinguished destruction of all ages, sexes and conditions.

In every stage of these Oppressions We have Petitioned for Redress in the most humble terms: Our repeated Petitions have been answered only by repeated injury. A Prince whose character is thus marked by every act which may define a Tyrant, is unfit to be the ruler of a free people.

Nor have We been wanting in attentions to our Brittish brethren. We have warned them from time to time of attempts by their legislature to extend an unwarrantable jurisdiction over us. We have reminded them of the circumstances of our emigration and settlement here. We have appealed to their native justice and magnanimity, and we have conjured them by the ties of our common kindred to disavow these usurpations, which, would inevitably interrupt our connections and correspondence. They too have been deaf to the voice of justice and of consanguinity. We must, therefore, acquiesce in the necessity, which denounces our Separation, and hold them, as we hold the rest of mankind, Enemies in War, in Peace Friends.

We, therefore, the Representatives of the united States of America, in General Congress, Assembled, appealing to the Supreme Judge of the world for the rectitude of our intentions, do, in the Name, and by Authority of the good People of these Colonies, solemnly publish and declare, That these United Colonies are, and of Right ought to be Free and Independent States; that they are Absolved from all Allegiance to the British Crown, and that all political connection between them and the State of Great Britain, is and ought to be totally dissolved; and that as Free and Independent States, they have full Power to levy War, conclude Peace, contract Alliances, establish Commerce, and to do all other Acts and Things which Independent States may of right do. And for the support of this Declaration, with a firm reliance on the protection of divine Providence, we mutually pledge to each other our Lives, our Fortunes and our sacred Honor.

The 56 signatures on the Declaration appear in the positions indicated:

COLUMN 1
Georgia:
Button Gwinnett
Lyman Hall
George Walton

COLUMN 2
North Carolina:
William Hooper
Joseph Hewes
John Penn
South Carolina:
Edward Rutledge
Thomas Heyward, Jr.
Thomas Lynch, Jr.
Arthur Middleton

COLUMN 3
Massachusetts:
John Hancock
Maryland:
Samuel Chase
William Paca
Thomas Stone
Charles Carroll of Carrollton
Virginia:
George Wythe
Richard Henry Lee
Thomas Jefferson
Benjamin Harrison
Thomas Nelson, Jr.
Francis Lightfoot Lee
Carter Braxton

COLUMN 4
Pennsylvania:
Robert Morris
Benjamin Rush
Benjamin Franklin
John Morton
George Clymer
James Smith
George Taylor
James Wilson
George Ross
Delaware:
Caesar Rodney
George Read
Thomas McKean

COLUMN 5
New York:
William Floyd
Philip Livingston
Francis Lewis
Lewis Morris
New Jersey:
Richard Stockton
John Witherspoon
Francis Hopkinson
John Hart
Abraham Clark

COLUMN 6
New Hampshire:
Josiah Bartlett
William Whipple

Massachusetts:
Samuel Adams
John Adams
Robert Treat Paine
Elbridge Gerry
Rhode Island:
Stephen Hopkins
William Ellery
Connecticut:
Roger Sherman
Samuel Huntington
William Williams
Oliver Wolcott
New Hampshire:
Matthew Thornton

The Constitution of the United States

Note: The following text is a transcription of the Constitution in its original form.
Items that are underlined have since been amended or superseded.

We the People of the United States, in Order to form a more perfect Union, establish Justice, insure domestic Tranquility, provide for the common defence, promote the general Welfare, and secure the Blessings of Liberty to ourselves and our Posterity, do ordain and establish this Constitution for the United States of America.

Article. I.

Section. 1.

All legislative Powers herein granted shall be vested in a Congress of the United States, which shall consist of a Senate and House of Representatives.

Section. 2.

The House of Representatives shall be composed of Members chosen every second Year by the People of the several States, and the Electors in each State shall have the Qualifications requisite for Electors of the most numerous Branch of the State Legislature.

No Person shall be a Representative who shall not have attained to the Age of twenty five Years, and been seven Years a Citizen of the United States, and who shall not, when elected, be an Inhabitant of that State in which he shall be chosen.

Representatives and direct Taxes shall be apportioned among the several States which may be included within this Union, according to their respective Numbers, which shall be determined by adding to the whole Number of free Persons, including those bound to Service for a Term of Years, and excluding Indians not taxed, three fifths of all other Persons. The actual Enumeration shall be made within three Years after the first Meeting of the Congress of the United States, and within every subsequent Term of ten Years, in such Manner as they shall by Law direct. The Number of Representatives shall not exceed one for every thirty Thousand, but each State shall have at Least one Representative; and until such enumeration shall be made, the State of New Hampshire shall be entitled to chuse three, Massachusetts eight, Rhode-Island and Providence Plantations one, Connecticut five, New-York six, New Jersey four, Pennsylvania eight, Delaware one, Maryland six, Virginia ten, North Carolina five, South Carolina five, and Georgia three.

When vacancies happen in the Representation from any State, the Executive Authority thereof shall issue Writs of Election to fill such Vacancies.

The House of Representatives shall chuse their Speaker and other Officers; and shall have the sole Power of Impeachment.

Section. 3.

The Senate of the United States shall be composed of two Senators from each State, chosen by the Legislature thereof for six Years; and each Senator shall have one Vote.

Immediately after they shall be assembled in Consequence of the first Election, they shall be divided as equally as may be into three Classes. The Seats of the Senators of the first Class shall be vacated at the Expiration of the second Year, of the second Class at the Expiration of the fourth Year, and of the third Class at the Expiration of the sixth Year, so that one third may be chosen every second Year; and if Vacancies happen by Resignation, or otherwise, during the Recess of the Legislature of any State, the Executive thereof may make temporary Appointments until the next Meeting of the Legislature, which shall then fill such Vacancies.

No Person shall be a Senator who shall not have attained to the Age of thirty Years, and been nine Years a Citizen of the United States, and who shall not, when elected, be an Inhabitant of that State for which he shall be chosen.

The Vice President of the United States shall be President of the Senate, but shall have no Vote, unless they be equally divided.

The Senate shall chuse their other Officers, and also a President pro tempore, in the Absence of the Vice President, or when he shall exercise the Office of President of the United States.

The Senate shall have the sole Power to try all Impeachments. When sitting for that Purpose, they shall be on Oath or Affirmation. When the

President of the United States is tried, the Chief Justice shall preside: And no Person shall be convicted without the Concurrence of two thirds of the Members present.

Judgment in Cases of Impeachment shall not extend further than to removal from Office, and disqualification to hold and enjoy any Office of honor, Trust or Profit under the United States: but the Party convicted shall nevertheless be liable and subject to Indictment, Trial, Judgment and Punishment, according to Law.

Section. 4.

The Times, Places and Manner of holding Elections for Senators and Representatives, shall be prescribed in each State by the Legislature thereof; but the Congress may at any time by Law make or alter such Regulations, except as to the Places of chusing Senators.

The Congress shall assemble at least once in every Year, and such Meeting shall be on the first Monday in December, unless they shall by Law appoint a different Day.

Section. 5.

Each House shall be the Judge of the Elections, Returns and Qualifications of its own Members, and a Majority of each shall constitute a Quorum to do Business; but a smaller Number may adjourn from day to day, and may be authorized to compel the Attendance of absent Members, in such Manner, and under such Penalties as each House may provide.

Each House may determine the Rules of its Proceedings, punish its Members for disorderly Behaviour, and, with the Concurrence of two thirds, expel a Member.

Each House shall keep a Journal of its Proceedings, and from time to time publish the same, excepting such Parts as may in their Judgment require Secrecy; and the Yeas and Nays of the Members of either House on any question shall, at the Desire of one fifth of those Present, be entered on the Journal.

Neither House, during the Session of Congress, shall, without the Consent of the other, adjourn for more than three days, nor to any other Place than that in which the two Houses shall be sitting.

Section. 6.

The Senators and Representatives shall receive a Compensation for their Services, to be ascertained by Law, and paid out of the Treasury of the United States. They shall in all Cases, except Treason, Felony and Breach of the Peace, be privileged from Arrest during their Attendance at the Session of their respective Houses, and in going to and returning from the same; and for any Speech or Debate in either House, they shall not be questioned in any other Place.

No Senator or Representative shall, during the Time for which he was elected, be appointed to any civil Office under the Authority of the United States, which shall have been created, or the Emoluments whereof shall have been encreased during such time; and no Person holding any Office under the United States, shall be a Member of either House during his Continuance in Office.

Section. 7.

All Bills for raising Revenue shall originate in the House of Representatives; but the Senate may propose or concur with Amendments as on other Bills.

Every Bill which shall have passed the House of Representatives and the Senate, shall, before it become a Law, be presented to the President of the United States: If he approve he shall sign it, but if not he shall return it, with his Objections to that House in which it shall have originated, who shall enter the Objections at large on their Journal, and proceed to reconsider it. If after such Reconsideration two thirds of that House shall agree to pass the Bill, it shall be sent, together with the Objections, to the other House, by which it shall likewise be reconsidered, and if approved by two thirds of that House, it shall become a Law. But in all such Cases the Votes of both Houses shall be determined by yeas and Nays, and the Names of the Persons voting for and against the Bill shall be entered on the Journal of each House respectively. If any Bill shall not be returned by the President within ten Days (Sundays excepted) after it shall have been presented to him, the Same shall be a Law, in like Manner as if he had signed it, unless the Congress by their Adjournment prevent its Return, in which Case it shall not be a Law.

Every Order, Resolution, or Vote to which the Concurrence of the Senate and House of Representatives may be necessary (except on a question of Adjournment) shall be presented to the President of the United States; and before the Same shall take Effect, shall be approved by him, or being disapproved by him, shall be repassed by two thirds of the Senate and House of Representatives, according to the Rules and Limitations prescribed in the Case of a Bill.

Section. 8.

The Congress shall have Power To lay and collect Taxes, Duties, Imposts and Excises, to pay the Debts and provide for the common Defence and general Welfare of the United States; but all Duties, Imposts and Excises shall be uniform throughout the United States;

To borrow Money on the credit of the United States;

To regulate Commerce with foreign Nations, and among the several States, and with the Indian Tribes;

To establish an uniform Rule of Naturalization, and uniform Laws on the subject of Bankruptcies throughout the United States;

To coin Money, regulate the Value thereof, and of foreign Coin, and fix the Standard of Weights and Measures;

To provide for the Punishment of counterfeiting the Securities and current Coin of the United States;

To establish Post Offices and post Roads;

To promote the Progress of Science and useful Arts, by securing for limited Times to Authors and Inventors the exclusive Right to their respective Writings and Discoveries;

To constitute Tribunals inferior to the supreme Court;

To define and punish Piracies and Felonies committed on the high Seas, and Offences against the Law of Nations;

To declare War, grant Letters of Marque and Reprisal, and make Rules concerning Captures on Land and Water;

To raise and support Armies, but no Appropriation of Money to that Use shall be for a longer Term than two Years;

To provide and maintain a Navy;

To make Rules for the Government and Regulation of the land and naval Forces;

To provide for calling forth the Militia to execute the Laws of the Union, suppress Insurrections and repel Invasions;

To provide for organizing, arming, and disciplining, the Militia, and for governing such Part of them as may be employed in the Service of the United States, reserving to the States respectively, the Appointment of the Officers, and the Authority of training the Militia according to the discipline prescribed by Congress;

To exercise exclusive Legislation in all Cases whatsoever, over such District (not exceeding ten Miles square) as may, by Cession of particular States, and the Acceptance of Congress, become the Seat of the Government of the United States, and to exercise like Authority over all Places purchased by the Consent of the Legislature of the State in which the Same shall be, for the Erection of Forts, Magazines, Arsenals, dock-Yards, and other needful Buildings;—And

To make all Laws which shall be necessary and proper for carrying into Execution the foregoing Powers, and all other Powers vested by this Constitution in the Government of the United States, or in any Department or Officer thereof.

Section. 9.

The Migration or Importation of such Persons as any of the States now existing shall think proper to admit, shall not be prohibited by the Congress prior to the Year one thousand eight hundred and eight, but a Tax or duty may be imposed on such Importation, not exceeding ten dollars for each Person.

The Privilege of the Writ of Habeas Corpus shall not be suspended, unless when in Cases of Rebellion or Invasion the public Safety may require it.

No Bill of Attainder or ex post facto Law shall be passed.

No Capitation, or other direct, Tax shall be laid, unless in Proportion to the Census or enumeration herein before directed to be taken.

No Tax or Duty shall be laid on Articles exported from any State.

No Preference shall be given by any Regulation of Commerce or Revenue to the Ports of one State over those of another; nor shall Vessels bound to, or from, one State, be obliged to enter, clear, or pay Duties in another.

No Money shall be drawn from the Treasury, but in Consequence of Appropriations made by Law; and a regular Statement and Account of the Receipts and Expenditures of all public Money shall be published from time to time.

No Title of Nobility shall be granted by the United States: And no Person holding any Office of Profit or Trust under them, shall, without the Consent of the Congress, accept of any present, Emolument, Office, or Title, of any kind whatever, from any King, Prince, or foreign State.

Section. 10.

No State shall enter into any Treaty, Alliance, or Confederation; grant Letters of Marque and Reprisal; coin Money; emit Bills of Credit; make any Thing but gold and silver Coin a Tender in Payment of Debts; pass any Bill of Attainder, ex post facto Law, or Law impairing the Obligation of Contracts, or grant any Title of Nobility.

No State shall, without the Consent of the Congress, lay any Imposts or Duties on Imports or Exports, except what may be absolutely necessary for executing it's inspection Laws: and the net Produce of all Duties and Imposts, laid by any State on Imports or Exports, shall be for the Use of the Treasury of the United States; and all such Laws shall be subject to the Revision and Controul of the Congress.

No State shall, without the Consent of Congress, lay any Duty of Tonnage, keep Troops, or Ships of War in time of Peace, enter into any Agreement or Compact with another State, or with a foreign Power, or engage in War, unless actually invaded, or in such imminent Danger as will not admit of delay.

ARTICLE. II.

Section. 1.

The executive Power shall be vested in a President of the United States of America. He shall hold his Office during the Term of four Years, and, together with the Vice President, chosen for the same Term, be elected, as follows:

Each State shall appoint, in such Manner as the Legislature thereof may direct, a Number of Electors, equal to the whole Number of Senators and Representatives to which the State may be entitled in the Congress: but no Senator or Representative, or Person holding an Office of Trust or Profit under the United States, shall be appointed an Elector.

The Electors shall meet in their respective States, and vote by Ballot for two Persons, of whom one at least shall not be an Inhabitant of the same State with themselves. And they shall make a List of all the Persons voted for, and of the Number of Votes for each; which List they shall sign and certify, and transmit sealed to the Seat of the Government of the United States, directed to the President of the Senate. The President of the Senate shall, in the Presence of the Senate and House of Representatives, open all the Certificates, and the Votes shall then be counted. The Person having the greatest Number of Votes shall be the President, if such Number be a Majority of the whole Number of Electors appointed; and if there be more than one who have such Majority, and have an equal Number of Votes, then the House of Representatives shall immediately chuse by Ballot one of them for President; and if no Person have a Majority, then from the five highest on the List the said House shall in like Manner chuse the President. But in chusing the President, the Votes shall be taken by States, the Representation from each State having one Vote; A quorum for this purpose shall consist of a Member or Members from two thirds of the States, and a Majority of all the States shall be necessary to a Choice. In every Case, after the Choice of the President, the Person having the greatest Number of Votes of the Electors shall be the Vice President. But if there should remain two or more who have equal Votes, the Senate shall chuse from them by Ballot the Vice President.

The Congress may determine the Time of chusing the Electors, and the Day on which they shall give their Votes; which Day shall be the same throughout the United States.

No Person except a natural born Citizen, or a Citizen of the United States, at the time of the Adoption of this Constitution, shall be eligible to the Office of President; neither shall any Person be eligible to that Office who shall not have attained to the Age of thirty five Years, and been fourteen Years a Resident within the United States.

In Case of the Removal of the President from Office, or of his Death, Resignation, or Inability to discharge the Powers and Duties of the said Office, the Same shall devolve on the Vice President, and the Congress may by Law provide for the Case of Removal, Death, Resignation or Inability, both of the President and Vice President, declaring what Officer shall then act as President, and such Officer shall act accordingly, until the Disability be removed, or a President shall be elected.

The President shall, at stated Times, receive for his Services, a Compensation, which shall neither be increased nor diminished during the Period for which he shall have been elected, and he shall not receive within that Period any other Emolument from the United States, or any of them.

Before he enter on the Execution of his Office, he shall take the following Oath or Affirmation:—"I do solemnly swear (or affirm) that I will faithfully execute the Office of President of the United States, and will to the best of my Ability, preserve, protect and defend the Constitution of the United States."

Section. 2.

The President shall be Commander in Chief of the Army and Navy of the United States, and of the Militia of the several States, when called into the actual Service of the United States; he may require the Opinion, in writing, of the principal Officer in each of the executive Departments, upon any Subject relating to the Duties of their respective Offices, and he shall have Power to grant Reprieves and Pardons for Offences against the United States, except in Cases of Impeachment.

He shall have Power, by and with the Advice and Consent of the Senate, to make Treaties, provided two thirds of the Senators present concur; and he shall nominate, and by and with the Advice and Consent of the Senate, shall appoint Ambassadors, other public Ministers and Consuls, Judges of the supreme Court, and all other Officers of the United States, whose Appointments are not herein otherwise provided for, and which shall be established by Law: but the Congress may by Law vest the Appointment of such inferior Officers, as they think proper, in the President alone, in the Courts of Law, or in the Heads of Departments.

The President shall have Power to fill up all Vacancies that may happen during the Recess of the Senate, by granting Commissions which shall expire at the End of their next Session.

Section. 3.

He shall from time to time give to the Congress Information of the State of the Union, and recommend to their Consideration such Measures as he shall judge necessary and expedient; he may, on extraordinary Occasions, convene both Houses, or either of them, and in Case of

Disagreement between them, with Respect to the Time of Adjournment, he may adjourn them to such Time as he shall think proper; he shall receive Ambassadors and other public Ministers; he shall take Care that the Laws be faithfully executed, and shall Commission all the Officers of the United States.

Section. 4.

The President, Vice President and all civil Officers of the United States, shall be removed from Office on Impeachment for, and Conviction of, Treason, Bribery, or other high Crimes and Misdemeanors.

ARTICLE III.

Section. 1.

The judicial Power of the United States shall be vested in one supreme Court, and in such inferior Courts as the Congress may from time to time ordain and establish. The Judges, both of the supreme and inferior Courts, shall hold their Offices during good Behaviour, and shall, at stated Times, receive for their Services a Compensation, which shall not be diminished during their Continuance in Office.

Section. 2.

The judicial Power shall extend to all Cases, in Law and Equity, arising under this Constitution, the Laws of the United States, and Treaties made, or which shall be made, under their Authority;—to all Cases affecting Ambassadors, other public Ministers and Consuls;—to all Cases of admiralty and maritime Jurisdiction;—to Controversies to which the United States shall be a Party;—to Controversies between two or more States;— between a State and Citizens of another State;—between Citizens of different States;—between Citizens of the same State claiming Lands under Grants of different States, and between a State, or the Citizens thereof, and foreign States, Citizens or Subjects.

In all Cases affecting Ambassadors, other public Ministers and Consuls, and those in which a State shall be Party, the supreme Court shall have original Jurisdiction. In all the other Cases before mentioned, the supreme Court shall have appellate Jurisdiction, both as to Law and Fact, with such Exceptions, and under such Regulations as the Congress shall make.

The Trial of all Crimes, except in Cases of Impeachment, shall be by Jury; and such Trial shall be held in the State where the said Crimes shall have been committed; but when not committed within any State, the Trial shall be at such Place or Places as the Congress may by Law have directed.

Section. 3.

Treason against the United States, shall consist only in levying War against them, or in adhering to their Enemies, giving them Aid and Comfort. No Person shall be convicted of Treason unless on the Testimony of two Witnesses to the same overt Act, or on Confession in open Court.

The Congress shall have Power to declare the Punishment of Treason, but no Attainder of Treason shall work Corruption of Blood, or Forfeiture except during the Life of the Person attainted.

ARTICLE. IV.

Section. 1.

Full Faith and Credit shall be given in each State to the public Acts, Records, and judicial Proceedings of every other State. And the Congress may by general Laws prescribe the Manner in which such Acts, Records and Proceedings shall be proved, and the Effect thereof.

Section. 2.

The Citizens of each State shall be entitled to all Privileges and Immunities of Citizens in the several States.

A Person charged in any State with Treason, Felony, or other Crime, who shall flee from Justice, and be found in another State, shall on Demand of the executive Authority of the State from which he fled, be delivered up, to be removed to the State having Jurisdiction of the Crime.

No Person held to Service or Labour in one State, under the Laws thereof, escaping into another, shall, in Consequence of any Law or Regulation therein, be discharged from such Service or Labour, but shall be delivered up on Claim of the Party to whom such Service or Labour may be due.

Section. 3.

New States may be admitted by the Congress into this Union; but no new State shall be formed or erected within the Jurisdiction of any other State; nor any State be formed by the Junction of two or more States, or Parts of States, without the Consent of the Legislatures of the States concerned as well as of the Congress.

The Congress shall have Power to dispose of and make all needful Rules and Regulations respecting the Territory or other Property belonging to the United States; and nothing in this Constitution shall be so construed as to Prejudice any Claims of the United States, or of any particular State.

Section. 4.

The United States shall guarantee to every State in this Union a Republican Form of Government, and shall protect each of them against Invasion; and on Application of the Legislature, or of the Executive (when the Legislature cannot be convened), against domestic Violence.

ARTICLE. V.

The Congress, whenever two thirds of both Houses shall deem it necessary, shall propose Amendments to this Constitution, or, on the Application of the Legislatures of two thirds of the several States, shall call a Convention for proposing Amendments, which, in either Case, shall be valid to all Intents and Purposes, as Part of this Constitution, when ratified by the Legislatures of three fourths of the several States, or by Conventions in three fourths thereof, as the one or the other Mode of Ratification may be proposed by the Congress; Provided that no Amendment which may be made prior to the Year One thousand eight hundred and eight shall in any Manner affect the first and fourth Clauses in the Ninth Section of the first Article; and that no State, without its Consent, shall be deprived of its equal Suffrage in the Senate.

ARTICLE. VI.

All Debts contracted and Engagements entered into, before the Adoption of this Constitution, shall be as valid against the United States under this Constitution, as under the Confederation.

This Constitution, and the Laws of the United States which shall be made in Pursuance thereof; and all Treaties made, or which shall be made, under the Authority of the United States, shall be the supreme Law of the Land; and the Judges in every State shall be bound thereby, any Thing in the Constitution or Laws of any State to the Contrary notwithstanding.

The Senators and Representatives before mentioned, and the Members of the several State Legislatures, and all executive and judicial Officers, both of the United States and of the several States, shall be bound by Oath or Affirmation, to support this Constitution; but no religious Test shall ever be required as a Qualification to any Office or public Trust under the United States.

ARTICLE. VII.

The Ratification of the Conventions of nine States, shall be sufficient for the Establishment of this Constitution between the States so ratifying the Same.

The Word, "the," being interlined between the seventh and eighth Lines of the first Page, the Word "Thirty" being partly written on an Erazure in the fifteenth Line of the first Page, The Words "is tried" being interlined between the thirty second and thirty third Lines of the first Page and the Word "the" being interlined between the forty third and forty fourth Lines of the second Page.

Attest William Jackson Secretary

Done in Convention by the Unanimous Consent of the States present the Seventeenth Day of September in the Year of our Lord one thousand seven hundred and Eighty seven and of the Independence of the United States of America the Twelfth In witness whereof We have hereunto subscribed our Names,

G⁰. Washington
Presidt and deputy from
Virginia

Delaware
Geo: Read
Gunning Bedford jun
John Dickinson
Richard Bassett
Jaco: Broom

Maryland
James McHenry
Dan of St Thos. Jenifer
Danl. Carroll

Virginia
John Blair
James Madison Jr.

North Carolina
Wm. Blount
Richd. Dobbs Spaight
Hu Williamson

South Carolina
J. Rutledge
Charles Cotesworth Pinckney
Charles Pinckney
Pierce Butler

Georgia
William Few
Abr Baldwin

New Hampshire
John Langdon
Nicholas Gilman

Massachusetts
Nathaniel Gorham
Rufus King

Connecticut
Wm. Saml. Johnson
Roger Sherman

New York
Alexander Hamilton

New Jersey
Wil: Livingston
David Brearley
Wm. Paterson
Jona: Dayton

Pennsylvania
B Franklin
Thomas Mifflin
Robt. Morris
Geo. Clymer
Thos. FitzSimons
Jared Ingersoll
James Wilson
Gouv Morris

The Bill of Rights

Note: The following text is a transcription of the first ten amendments to the Constitution in their original form. These amendments were ratified December 15, 1791, and form what is known as the "Bill of Rights."

Amendment I

Congress shall make no law respecting an establishment of religion, or prohibiting the free exercise thereof; or abridging the freedom of speech, or of the press; or the right of the people peaceably to assemble, and to petition the Government for a redress of grievances.

Amendment II

A well regulated Militia, being necessary to the security of a free State, the right of the people to keep and bear Arms, shall not be infringed.

Amendment III

No Soldier shall, in time of peace be quartered in any house, without the consent of the Owner, nor in time of war, but in a manner to be prescribed by law.

Amendment IV

The right of the people to be secure in their persons, houses, papers, and effects, against unreasonable searches and seizures, shall not be violated, and no Warrants shall issue, but upon probable cause, supported by Oath or affirmation, and particularly describing the place to be searched, and the persons or things to be seized.

Amendment V

No person shall be held to answer for a capital, or otherwise infamous crime, unless on a presentment or indictment of a Grand Jury, except in cases arising in the land or naval forces, or in the Militia, when in actual service in time of War or public danger; nor shall any person be subject for the same offence to be twice put in jeopardy of life or limb; nor shall be compelled in any criminal case to be a witness against himself, nor be deprived of life, liberty, or property, without due process of law; nor shall private property be taken for public use, without just compensation.

Amendment VI

In all criminal prosecutions, the accused shall enjoy the right to a speedy and public trial, by an impartial jury of the State and district wherein the crime shall have been committed, which district shall have been previously ascertained by law, and to be informed of the nature and cause of the accusation; to be confronted with the witnesses against him; to have compulsory process for obtaining witnesses in his favor, and to have the Assistance of Counsel for his defence.

Amendment VII

In Suits at common law, where the value in controversy shall exceed twenty dollars, the right of trial by jury shall be preserved, and no fact tried by a jury, shall be otherwise reexamined in any Court of the United States, than according to the rules of the common law.

Amendment VIII

Excessive bail shall not be required, nor excessive fines imposed, nor cruel and unusual punishments inflicted.

Amendment IX

The enumeration in the Constitution, of certain rights, shall not be construed to deny or disparage others retained by the people.

Amendment X

The powers not delegated to the United States by the Constitution, nor prohibited by it to the States, are reserved to the States respectively, or to the people.

Note: The capitalization and punctuation in this version is from the enrolled original of the Joint Resolution of Congress proposing the Bill of Rights, which is on permanent display in the Rotunda of the National Archives Building, Washington, D.C.

The Constitution: Amendments 11–27

Constitutional Amendments 1–10 make up what is known as The Bill of Rights.

Amendments 11–27 are listed below.

Amendment XI

Passed by Congress March 4, 1794. Ratified February 7, 1795.

Note: Article III, section 2, of the Constitution was modified by amendment 11.

The Judicial power of the United States shall not be construed to extend to any suit in law or equity, commenced or prosecuted against one of the United States by Citizens of another State, or by Citizens or Subjects of any Foreign State.

Amendment XII

Passed by Congress December 9, 1803. Ratified June 15, 1804.

Note: A portion of Article II, section 1 of the Constitution was superseded by the 12th amendment.

The Electors shall meet in their respective states and vote by ballot for President and Vice-President, one of whom, at least, shall not be an inhabitant of the same state with themselves; they shall name in their ballots the person voted for as President, and in distinct ballots the person voted for as Vice-President, and they shall make distinct lists of all persons voted for as President, and of all persons voted for as Vice-President, and of the number of votes for each, which lists they shall sign and certify, and transmit sealed to the seat of the government of the United States, directed to the President of the Senate; — the President of the Senate shall, in the presence of the Senate and House of Representatives, open all the certificates and the votes shall then be counted; — The person having the greatest number of votes for President, shall be the President, if such number be a majority of the whole number of Electors appointed; and if no person have such majority, then from the persons having the highest numbers not exceeding three on the list of those voted for as President, the House of Representatives shall choose immediately, by ballot, the President. But in choosing the President, the votes shall be taken by states, the representation from each state having one vote; a quorum for this purpose shall consist of a member or members from two-thirds of the states, and a majority of all the states shall be necessary to a choice. [And if the House of Representatives shall not choose a President whenever the right of choice shall devolve upon them, before the fourth day of March next following, then the Vice-President shall act as President, as in case of the death or other constitutional disability of the President. —]* The person having the greatest number of votes as Vice-President, shall be the Vice-President, if such number be a majority of the whole number of Electors appointed, and if no person have a majority, then from the two highest numbers on the list, the Senate shall choose the Vice-President; a quorum for the purpose shall consist of two-thirds of the whole number of Senators, and a majority of the whole number shall be necessary to a choice. But no person constitutionally ineligible to the office of President shall be eligible to that of Vice-President of the United States.

Superseded by section 3 of the 20th amendment.

Amendment XIII

Passed by Congress January 31, 1865. Ratified December 6, 1865.

Note: A portion of Article IV, section 2, of the Constitution was superseded by the 13th amendment.

Section 1.
Neither slavery nor involuntary servitude, except as a punishment for crime whereof the party shall have been duly convicted, shall exist within the United States, or any place subject to their jurisdiction.

Section 2.
Congress shall have power to enforce this article by appropriate legislation.

Amendment XIV

Passed by Congress June 13, 1866. Ratified July 9, 1868.

Note: Article I, section 2, of the Constitution was modified by section 2 of the 14th amendment.

Section 1.
All persons born or naturalized in the United States, and subject to the jurisdiction thereof, are citizens of the United States and of the State wherein they reside. No State shall make or enforce any law which shall abridge the privileges or immunities of citizens of the United States; nor shall any State deprive any person of life, liberty, or property, without due process of law; nor deny to any person within its jurisdiction the equal protection of the laws.

Section 2.
Representatives shall be apportioned among the several States according to their respective numbers, counting the whole number of persons in each State, excluding Indians not taxed. But when the right to vote at any election for the choice of electors for President and

Vice-President of the United States, Representatives in Congress, the Executive and Judicial officers of a State, or the members of the Legislature thereof, is denied to any of the male inhabitants of such State, being twenty-one years of age,* and citizens of the United States, or in any way abridged, except for participation in rebellion, or other crime, the basis of representation therein shall be reduced in the proportion which the number of such male citizens shall bear to the whole number of male citizens twenty-one years of age in such State.

Section 3.

No person shall be a Senator or Representative in Congress, or elector of President and Vice-President, or hold any office, civil or military, under the United States, or under any State, who, having previously taken an oath, as a member of Congress, or as an officer of the United States, or as a member of any State legislature, or as an executive or judicial officer of any State, to support the Constitution of the United States, shall have engaged in insurrection or rebellion against the same, or given aid or comfort to the enemies thereof. But Congress may by a vote of two-thirds of each House, remove such disability.

Section 4.

The validity of the public debt of the United States, authorized by law, including debts incurred for payment of pensions and bounties for services in suppressing insurrection or rebellion, shall not be questioned. But neither the United States nor any State shall assume or pay any debt or obligation incurred in aid of insurrection or rebellion against the United States, or any claim for the loss or emancipation of any slave; but all such debts, obligations and claims shall be held illegal and void.

Section 5.

The Congress shall have the power to enforce, by appropriate legislation, the provisions of this article.

*Changed by section 1 of the 26th amendment.

Amendment XV

Passed by Congress February 26, 1869. Ratified February 3, 1870.

Section 1.
The right of citizens of the United States to vote shall not be denied or abridged by the United States or by any State on account of race, color, or previous condition of servitude—

Section 2.
The Congress shall have the power to enforce this article by appropriate legislation.

Amendment XVI

Passed by Congress July 2, 1909. Ratified February 3, 1913.

Note: Article I, section 9, of the Constitution was modified by amendment 16.

The Congress shall have power to lay and collect taxes on incomes, from whatever source derived, without apportionment among the several States, and without regard to any census or enumeration.

Amendment XVII

Passed by Congress May 13, 1912. Ratified April 8, 1913.

Note: Article I, section 3, of the Constitution was modified by the 17th amendment.

The Senate of the United States shall be composed of two Senators from each State, elected by the people thereof, for six years; and each Senator shall have one vote. The electors in each State shall have the qualifications requisite for electors of the most numerous branch of the State legislatures.

When vacancies happen in the representation of any State in the Senate, the executive authority of such State shall issue writs of election to fill such vacancies: Provided, That the legislature of any State may empower the executive thereof to make temporary appointments until the people fill the vacancies by election as the legislature may direct.

This amendment shall not be so construed as to affect the election or term of any Senator chosen before it becomes valid as part of the Constitution.

AMENDMENT XVIII

Passed by Congress December 18, 1917. Ratified January 16, 1919. Repealed by amendment 21.

Section 1.

After one year from the ratification of this article the manufacture, sale, or transportation of intoxicating liquors within, the importation thereof into, or the exportation thereof from the United States and all territory subject to the jurisdiction thereof for beverage purposes is hereby prohibited.

Section 2.

The Congress and the several States shall have concurrent power to enforce this article by appropriate legislation.

Section 3.

This article shall be inoperative unless it shall have been ratified as an amendment to the Constitution by the legislatures of the several States, as provided in the Constitution, within seven years from the date of the submission hereof to the States by the Congress.

AMENDMENT XIX

Passed by Congress June 4, 1919. Ratified August 18, 1920.

The right of citizens of the United States to vote shall not be denied or abridged by the United States or by any State on account of sex.

Congress shall have power to enforce this article by appropriate legislation.

Amendment XX

Passed by Congress March 2, 1932. Ratified January 23, 1933.

Note: Article I, section 4, of the Constitution was modified by section 2 of this amendment. In addition, a portion of the 12th amendment was superseded by section 3.

Section 1.
The terms of the President and the Vice President shall end at noon on the 20th day of January, and the terms of Senators and Representatives at noon on the 3d day of January, of the years in which such terms would have ended if this article had not been ratified; and the terms of their successors shall then begin.

Section 2.
The Congress shall assemble at least once in every year, and such meeting shall begin at noon on the 3d day of January, unless they shall by law appoint a different day.

Section 3.
If, at the time fixed for the beginning of the term of the President, the President elect shall have died, the Vice President elect shall become President. If a President shall not have been chosen before the time fixed for the beginning of his term, or if the President elect shall have failed to qualify, then the Vice President elect shall act as President until a President shall have qualified; and the Congress may by law provide for the case wherein neither a President elect nor a Vice President shall have qualified, declaring who shall then act as President, or the manner in which one who is to act shall be selected, and such person shall act accordingly until a President or Vice President shall have qualified.

Section 4.

The Congress may by law provide for the case of the death of any of the persons from whom the House of Representatives may choose a President whenever the right of choice shall have devolved upon them, and for the case of the death of any of the persons from whom the Senate may choose a Vice President whenever the right of choice shall have devolved upon them.

Section 5.

Sections 1 and 2 shall take effect on the 15th day of October following the ratification of this article.

Section 6.

This article shall be inoperative unless it shall have been ratified as an amendment to the Constitution by the legislatures of three-fourths of the several States within seven years from the date of its submission.

Amendment XXI

Passed by Congress February 20, 1933. Ratified December 5, 1933.

Section 1.

The eighteenth article of amendment to the Constitution of the United States is hereby repealed.

Section 2.

The transportation or importation into any State, Territory, or Possession of the United States for delivery or use therein of intoxicating liquors, in violation of the laws thereof, is hereby prohibited.

Section 3.

This article shall be inoperative unless it shall have been ratified as an amendment to the Constitution by conventions in the several States, as provided in the Constitution, within seven years from the date of the submission hereof to the States by the Congress.

Amendment XXII

Passed by Congress March 21, 1947. Ratified February 27, 1951.

Section 1.
No person shall be elected to the office of the President more than twice, and no person who has held the office of President, or acted as President, for more than two years of a term to which some other person was elected President shall be elected to the office of President more than once. But this Article shall not apply to any person holding the office of President when this Article was proposed by Congress, and shall not prevent any person who may be holding the office of President, or acting as President, during the term within which this Article becomes operative from holding the office of President or acting as President during the remainder of such term.

Section 2.
This article shall be inoperative unless it shall have been ratified as an amendment to the Constitution by the legislatures of three-fourths of the several States within seven years from the date of its submission to the States by the Congress.

Amendment XXIII

Passed by Congress June 16, 1960. Ratified March 29, 1961.

Section 1.
The District constituting the seat of Government of the United States shall appoint in such manner as Congress may direct:
A number of electors of President and Vice President equal to the whole number of Senators and Representatives in Congress to which the District would be entitled if it were a State, but in no event more than the least populous State; they shall be in addition to those appointed by the States, but they shall be considered, for the purposes of the election of President and Vice President, to be electors appointed by a State; and they shall meet in the District and perform such duties as provided by the twelfth article of amendment.

Section 2.

The Congress shall have power to enforce this article by appropriate legislation.

AMENDMENT XXIV

Passed by Congress August 27, 1962. Ratified January 23, 1964.

Section 1.

The right of citizens of the United States to vote in any primary or other election for President or Vice President, for electors for President or Vice President, or for Senator or Representative in Congress, shall not be denied or abridged by the United States or any State by reason of failure to pay poll tax or other tax.

Section 2.

The Congress shall have power to enforce this article by appropriate legislation.

AMENDMENT XXV

Passed by Congress July 6, 1965. Ratified February 10, 1967.

Note: Article II, section 1, of the Constitution was affected by the 25th amendment.

Section 1.

In case of the removal of the President from office or of his death or resignation, the Vice President shall become President.

Section 2.

Whenever there is a vacancy in the office of the Vice President, the President shall nominate a Vice President who shall take office upon confirmation by a majority vote of both Houses of Congress.

Section 3.

Whenever the President transmits to the President pro tempore of the Senate and the Speaker of the House of Representatives his written declaration that he is unable to discharge the powers and duties of his office, and until he transmits to them a written declaration to the contrary, such powers and duties shall be discharged by the Vice President as Acting President.

Section 4.
Whenever the Vice President and a majority of either the principal officers of the executive departments or of such other body as Congress may by law provide, transmit to the President pro tempore of the Senate and the Speaker of the House of Representatives their written declaration that the President is unable to discharge the powers and duties of his office, the Vice President shall immediately assume the powers and duties of the office as Acting President.

Thereafter, when the President transmits to the President pro tempore of the Senate and the Speaker of the House of Representatives his written declaration that no inability exists, he shall resume the powers and duties of his office unless the Vice President and a majority of either the principal officers of the executive department or of such other body as Congress may by law provide, transmit within four days to the President pro tempore of the Senate and the Speaker of the House of Representatives their written declaration that the President is unable to discharge the powers and duties of his office. Thereupon Congress shall decide the issue, assembling within forty-eight hours for that purpose if not in session. If the Congress, within twenty-one days after receipt of the latter written declaration, or, if Congress is not in session, within twenty-one days after Congress is required to assemble, determines by two-thirds vote of both Houses that the President is unable to discharge the powers and duties of his office, the Vice President shall continue to discharge the same as Acting President; otherwise, the President shall resume the powers and duties of his office.

Amendment XXVI

Passed by Congress March 23, 1971. Ratified July 1, 1971.

Note: Amendment 14, section 2, of the Constitution was modified by section 1 of the 26th amendment.

Section 1.

The right of citizens of the United States, who are eighteen years of age or older, to vote shall not be denied or abridged by the United States or by any State on account of age.

Section 2.

The Congress shall have power to enforce this article by appropriate legislation.

Amendment XXVII

Originally proposed Sept. 25, 1789. Ratified May 7, 1992.

No law, varying the compensation for the services of the Senators and Representatives, shall take effect, until an election of representatives shall have intervened.

Appendix B: Authorizing Statutes for the Armed Forces

U.S. Army

TITLE 10, Subtitle B, PART I, CHAPTER 307.
Sec. 3062. – Policy; composition; organized peace establishment

(a) It is the intent of Congress to provide an Army that is capable, in conjunction with the other armed forces, of –

(1) preserving the peace and security, and providing for the defense, of the United States, the Territories, Commonwealths, and possessions, and any areas occupied by the United States;
(2) supporting the national policies;
(3) implementing the national objectives; and
(4) overcoming any nations responsible for aggressive acts that imperil the peace and security of the United States.

(b) In general, the Army, within the Department of the Army, includes land combat and service forces and such aviation and water transport as may be organic therein. It shall be organized, trained, and equipped primarily for prompt and sustained combat incident to operations on land. It is responsible for the preparation of land forces necessary for the effective prosecution of war except as otherwise assigned and, in accordance with integrated joint mobilization plans, for the expansion of the peacetime components of the Army to meet the needs of war.

(c) The Army consists of –

(1) the Regular Army, the Army National Guard of the United States, the Army National Guard while in the service of the United States and the Army Reserve; and
(2) all persons appointed or enlisted in, or conscripted into, the Army without component.

(d) The organized peace establishment of the Army consists of all –

(1) military organizations of the Army with their installations and supporting and auxiliary elements, including combat, training, administrative, and logistic elements; and
(2) members of the Army, including those not assigned to units; necessary to form the basis for a complete and immediate mobilization for the national defense in the event of a national emergency.

U.S. MARINE CORPS

TITLE 10, Subtitle C, PART I, CHAPTER 507.
Sec. 5063. – United States Marine Corps: composition; functions

(a) The Marine Corps, within the Department of the Navy, shall be so organized as to include not less than three combat divisions and three air wings, and such other land combat, aviation, and other services as may be organic therein. The Marine Corps shall be organized, trained, and equipped to provide fleet marine forces of combined arms, together with supporting air components, for service with the fleet in the seizure or defense of advanced naval bases and for the conduct of such land operations as may be essential to the prosecution of a naval campaign. In addition, the Marine Corps shall provide detachments and organizations for service on armed vessels of the Navy, shall provide security detachments for the protection of naval property at naval stations and bases, and shall perform such other duties as the President may direct. However, these additional duties may not detract from or interfere with the operations for which the Marine Corps is primarily organized.

(b) The Marine Corps shall develop, in coordination with the Army and the Air Force, those phases of amphibious operations that pertain to the tactics, technique, and equipment used by landing forces.

(c) The Marine Corps is responsible, in accordance with integrated joint mobilization plans, for the expansion of peacetime components of the Marine Corps to meet the needs of war.

U.S. Navy

TITLE 10, Subtitle C, PART I, CHAPTER 507.
Sec. 5062. – United States Navy: composition; functions

(a) The Navy, within the Department of the Navy, includes, in general, naval combat and service forces and such aviation as may be organic therein. The Navy shall be organized, trained, and equipped primarily for prompt and sustained combat incident to operations at sea. It is responsible for the preparation of naval forces necessary for the effective prosecution of war except as otherwise assigned and, in accordance with integrated joint mobilization plans, for the expansion of the peacetime components of the Navy to meet the needs of war.

(b) All naval aviation shall be integrated with the naval service as part thereof within the Department of the Navy. Naval aviation consists of combat and service and training forces, and includes land-based naval aviation, air transport essential for naval operations, all air weapons and air techniques involved in the operations and activities of the Navy, and the entire remainder of the aeronautical organization of the Navy, together with the personnel necessary therefor.

(c) The Navy shall develop aircraft, weapons, tactics, technique, organization, and equipment of naval combat and service elements. Matters of joint concern as to these functions shall be coordinated between the Army, the Air Force, and the Navy.

U.S. Air Force

TITLE 10, Subtitle D, PART I, CHAPTER 807.
Sec. 8062. – Policy; composition; aircraft authorization

(a) It is the intent of Congress to provide an Air Force that is capable, in conjunction with the other armed forces, of –

(1) preserving the peace and security, and providing for the defense, of the United States, the Territories, Commonwealths, and possessions, and any areas occupied by the United States;
(2) supporting the national policies;
(3) implementing the national objectives; and
(4) overcoming any nations responsible for aggressive acts that imperil the peace and security of the United States.

(b) There is a United States Air Force within the Department of the Air Force.

(c) In general, the Air Force includes aviation forces both combat and service not otherwise assigned. It shall be organized, trained, and equipped primarily for prompt and sustained offensive and defensive air operations. It is responsible for the preparation of the air forces necessary for the effective prosecution of war except as otherwise assigned and, in accordance with integrated joint mobilization plans, for the expansion of the peacetime components of the Air Force to meet the needs of war.

(d) The Air Force consists of –

(1) the Regular Air Force, the Air National Guard of the United States, the Air National Guard while in the service of the United States, and the Air Force Reserve;

(2) all persons appointed or enlisted in, or conscripted into, the Air Force without component; and

(3) all Air Force units and other Air Force organizations, with their installations and supporting and auxiliary combat, training, administrative, and logistic elements; and all members of the Air Force, including those not assigned to units; necessary to form the basis for a complete and immediate mobilization for the national defense in the event of a national emergency.

(e) Subject to subsection (f) of this section, chapter 831 of this title, and the strength authorized by law pursuant to section 115 of this title, the authorized strength of the Air Force is 70 Regular Air Force groups and such separate Regular Air Force squadrons, reserve groups, and supporting and auxiliary regular and reserve units as required.

(f) There are authorized for the Air Force 24,000 serviceable aircraft or 225,000 airframe tons of serviceable aircraft, whichever the Secretary of the Air Force considers appropriate to carry out this section. This subsection does not apply to guided missiles.

U.S. Coast Guard

TITLE 14, PART I, CHAPTER 1.
Sec. 1. – Establishment of Coast Guard

The Coast Guard as established January 28, 1915, shall be a military service and a branch of the armed forces of the United States at all times. The Coast Guard shall be a service in the Department of Homeland Security, except when operating as a service in the Navy.

Sec. 2. – Primary duties

The Coast Guard shall enforce or assist in the enforcement of all applicable Federal laws on, under, and over the high seas and waters subject to the jurisdiction of the United States; shall engage in maritime air surveillance or interdiction to enforce or assist in the enforcement of the laws of the United States; shall administer laws and promulgate and enforce regulations for the promotion of safety of life and property on and under the high seas and waters subject to the jurisdiction of the United States covering all matters not specifically delegated by law to some other executive department; shall develop, establish, maintain, and operate, with due regard to the requirements of national defense, aids to maritime navigation, ice-breaking facilities, and rescue facilities for the promotion of safety on, under, and over the high seas and waters subject to the jurisdiction of the United States; shall, pursuant to international agreements, develop, establish, maintain, and operate icebreaking facilities on, under, and over waters other than the high seas and waters subject to the jurisdiction of the United States; shall engage in oceanographic research of the high seas and in waters subject to the jurisdiction of the United States; and shall maintain a state of readiness to function as a specialized service in the Navy in time of war, including the fulfillment of Maritime Defense Zone command responsibilities.

Appendix C: Service Values of the Armed Forces

U.S. ARMY
Loyalty
Duty
Respect
Selfless Service
Honor
Integrity
Personal Courage

U.S. NAVY AND MARINE CORPS
Honor
Courage
Commitment

U.S. AIR FORCE
Integrity First
Service Before Self
Excellence in All We Do

U.S. COAST GUARD
Honor
Respect
Devotion to Duty

Appendix D: Code of Conduct for Members of the United States Armed Forces

I

I am an American, fighting in the forces which guard my country and our way of life. I am prepared to give my life in their defense.

II

I will never surrender of my own free will. If in command, I will never surrender the members of my command while they still have the means to resist.

III

If I am captured I will continue to resist by all means available. I will make every effort to escape and aid others to escape. I will accept neither parole nor special favors from the enemy.

IV

If I become a prisoner of war, I will keep faith with my fellow prisoners. I will give no information or take part in any action which might be harmful to my comrades. If I am senior, I will take command. If not, I will obey the lawful orders of those appointed over me and will back them up in every way.

V

When questioned, should I become a prisoner of war, I am required to give name, rank, service number and date of birth. I will evade answering further questions to the utmost of my ability. I will make no oral or written statements disloyal to my country and its allies or harmful to their cause.

VI

I will never forget that I am an American, fighting for freedom, responsible for my actions, and dedicated to the principles which made my country free. I will trust in my God and in the United States of America.

Executive Order 10631 (1955) as amended by EO 11382 (1967) and EO 12633 (1988)

Notes

Notes

Notes

Notes